GROWING WITH BLOCKCHAIN

FROM INNOVATIVE POTENTIAL TO OPERATIONAL REALITY

Growing with Blockchain: From innovative potential to operational reality

Published by Novaro Publishing Ltd, Techno Park, Coventry University Technology Park, Puma Way, Coventry CV1 2TT
e: publish@novaropublishing.com.

ISBN: 978-1-8380674-0-3
E-ISBN: 978-1-8380674-1-0

British Library Cataloguing-in-Publication Data
A catalogue record for this book is available from the British Library.

Designed by Chantel Barnett, Clear Design CC Ltd.
www.designisclear.co.uk

For further details about our authors and our titles, see
www.novaropublishing.com.

GROWING WITH BLOCKCHAIN

FROM INNOVATIVE POTENTIAL TO OPERATIONAL REALITY

CONSULTANT EDITOR

KEVIN R SMITH

CONSULTANT EDITOR

Kevin R Smith is a business mentor, a blockchain influencer and a cryptocurrency CEO. Based on 30 years of practical experience in opening up new markets, raising finance and launching ventures, Kevin gives an inside view of how to realize the disruptive potential of blockchain in practice. His focus is on the questions that entrepreneurs, innovators and executives will be asking about how to gain an advantage and transform their operations. Kevin is currently mentoring blockchain ventures at the NatWest Accelerator and is chief executive of the blockchain and cryptocurrency advisory platform, CryptoPi. He is the founding partner of Boom & Partners.

CONTENTS

FOREWORD

One thing that every successful business leader knows and understands is the need to continue to learn and retain an open mind. More than that, they must ensure that their business, whether small or large, moves with the times and stays at the forefront of innovation. Learning without fear of investigating ideas and trying new technologies is central to the question of how a business grows and succeeds.

In recent years the speed of change has continued to accelerate, and with it the speed at which any company must adapt to new challenges and opportunities. Just as we at Cass Business School have adapted our courses and delivery techniques to reflect new opportunities in business then so too must business leaders adapt to new technology and possibilities.

As the new order replaces the old, those at the vanguard will grow whilst those who are too slow to learn and adapt will be left behind to wither and die. Blockchain is one such technology that has the power to revolutionize everything from supply chains to trade finance, and from payments to asset ownership, all whilst reducing costs but increasing efficiency and safety.

Whilst some are not aware of what exactly blockchain is and what it can do, and others remain sceptical for no other reason than that they do not fully understand how it works, there is no doubt that it is being used more every day and that it has already turned from disruptive potential to operational reality.

Every successful business leader owes it to themselves and their business to ensure that they learn, adapt and accept new technologies. Especially so now, as we emerge into the 'new normal' after lockdown and survival of the fittest will never have been more true.

This book gives great insight into options and actions for transforming performance with blockchain and how best to ensue that your business will grow and thrive.

DR STEFANIA ZERBINATI

As associate professor in entrepreneurship at Cass Business School and founder of the Museum of Entrepreneurship, Stefania has been researching and teaching entrepreneurship for over 15 years, as well as working directly with entrepreneurs at different stages of their development across several industries.

1.

BLOCKCHAIN AND THE
INVENTION OF DIGITAL TRUST

Robert Learney at Digital Catapult reports on why blockchain represents such a radical development in computer science and on how the trust machines it creates are being deployed

'I've developed a new open source P2P e-cash system called bitcoin. It's completely decentralized with no central server or trusted parties, because everything is based on crypto proof instead of trust. Give it a try or take a look at the screenshots and design paper.'

It was with these words that Satoshi Nakamoto revealed the invention of blockchain to the world on 11 February 2009. As you'll hear from many different sources, the blockchain created the first way for people to exchange or transfer value over the internet without a trusted third party. It's called 'the trust machine' for this very reason: before blockchain, no trust without third parties; after blockchain, suddenly a way that both you and I alone can agree that what we see written in front of us is the incorruptible truth and that, yes, I did send you those five bitcoins, bananas, invoices or whatever.

But Satoshi didn't work in a vacuum. His (her? their?) breakthrough actually required nearly 70 years of groundwork, combining the wisdom of hundreds of computer scientists and advanced mathematicians from nearly every corner of the world. It's this journey from there to here that makes blockchain even more revolutionary and sets the scene for any discussions of its future.

The trust machine

So what exactly makes blockchain a trust machine? Without repeating lengthy explanations of hash functions and elliptic curve cryptography, the basics are as follows. You and I both agree to use a notice board to post messages. But if I post a message to tell you I've sent you five apples and also try to post one telling Mrs Smith that I've sent her three of those same apples, the notice board sees me trying to lie and stops me. In fact, it all depends on which message it accepts first: the five apples to you or the three to Mrs Smith. In either event, I can't try to lie to the notice board, which means I can't lie to you (or to Mrs Smith).

So how is this different from us all agreeing to use something like a spreadsheet stored in a cloud database, where we each have the right levels of permission to read and write? It's a perceptive question. In many ways, it would look and feel much the same to you as a user. But in some deeply fundamental ways, a blockchain is completely different. With a blockchain you don't need to trust the company running the cloud storage that they will keep the system up and maintain its audit trail or that they hadn't made some secret changes to the software so that Mrs Smith always gets one extra apple.

In fact, while cloud databases might not explicitly use blockchain, they do make use of some of the same concepts that led to the creation of blockchain.

From the beginning

The first computers built in the 1940s were isolated, standalone systems consuming the power of a whole house. Invented for war, these first machines were set to tasks such as cracking ciphers and calculating artillery trajectories. It wasn't until 1951 that computers were used for civilian purposes (for tabulating the 1950 US census).

The 1950s saw developments in miniaturization, storage media and initial uptake of computing machines by the business community, but most importantly for the history of blockchain, the invention of the modem by the US Air Force in 1953. Computers could now communicate over normal voice lines rather than telegraph or special purpose data lines.

Making use of modems, telephone lines and teleprinters, the US military embarked on a project called Sage (semi-automated ground equipment) that used a series of massive computer centres (in fact, the largest physical computers ever built) to co-ordinate military radar data from across the US into a unified picture of US airspace to defend against Soviet nuclear strikes. From 1958 to 1966, 22 Sage centres were built and they remained operational – vacuum tube computers and all – until the 1980s.

Things then progressed rapidly throughout the 1960s with the creation of new programming languages, the invention and first use of integrated circuits, and new storage media. But most importantly for us, networking developed to the point of allowing people to log in to large central computers using remote terminals in a hub-and-spoke model. Note that the computers themselves weren't yet networked, but users could post messages to each other using the precursors of email and bulletin boards.

True inter-networking had to wait until October 1969 with the activation of the ARPAnet, the forerunner to the internet. For the first time, tens of computers across the continental US could share messages over a common network using a standardized protocol. This grew to hundreds of computers and soon reached beyond the US into Europe via transatlantic links. The rest, as they say, is history.

But there is one more important parallel invention which opened a new line of thinking which we need to explore first. The database. It may seem trivial. After all, people have been storing data for thousands of years in many forms. But the creation of digital databases didn't take place until the 1960s. Interestingly, one of the earliest databases evolved directly from the US military's Sage programme to serve bookings and reservations for American Airlines. Installed in 1964, the Sabre system (semi-automated business research environment) used two IBM mainframe computers and could handle 84,000 queries per day. The 1970s through to the 1980s then saw the development of more recognisable relational database systems such as SQL.

The birth of distributed computing

The combination of databases and networking led to the invention of distributed computing as its own branch of computer science in the 1970s. Distributed computing is exactly what it says: a method of dividing up or co-ordinating computational tasks between multiple physically separated systems or nodes.

When you think about reconciling databases, it is exactly what you need to do. You and I both need to make sure that the database telling me how many apples I have matches your copy exactly. The data we're sharing is known as the state of our system. Our computers have to communicate with each other to update the numbers of apples on our databases (state) and we have to make sure that neither one of us can let our copies fall out of synchronization with each other or one of us might try to sell the same apples twice. This is the nature of consensus: our two systems are marching in lockstep with each other.

At first it might seem obvious that you should connect multiple computers in a way that has one master computer co-ordinating the activities of a large collection of subsidiary systems to update their databases and manage computations. This is the classical client-server architecture, but it will fail if the master computer misbehaves. It could be misbehaving on purpose due to malicious code or it could be because a cosmic ray flipped a bit in memory and now the system is off running in its own little world. Either way, you have to trust absolutely in the stability and availability of the master.

So instead, let's make every node holding a replica of our database capable of behaving as both a client and a server, a so-called peer-to-peer architecture. We'll get a much more resilient system as a whole, because now any single node can misbehave while the rest should be able to carry on as normal.

The byzantine grandparents of blockchain

But the problem was that nobody at the time knew how to build peer-to-peer systems in a way that they could detect and respond to unexpected errors while still passing and recording real messages correctly. This actually remained an unsolved head-scratcher through to the late 1970s when the first major breakthrough occurred in distributed computing.

The problem with unexpected errors is just that: they're unexpected. Some error types can be predicted and controlled. But if something unexpected happens, like a cosmic ray flipping the wrong bit in memory, one peer computer could send out two contradictory messages to the rest of the network. So how does a node detect this type of fault and manage it?

This type of fault became known as a byzantine fault as a result of NASA-funded work undertaken in 1978 and formally published in 1982 as *The Byzantine Generals' Problem* by three leading computer scientists of the time. Thus began the race to develop ever better byzantine fault tolerant (BFT) consensus algorithms over the next decade, with obvious benefits for mission-critical systems in aircraft and military applications. In fact, every time you fly, you put your trust in BFT systems.

The next large breakthrough came in 1999 with the development of the practical byzantine fault tolerant (PBFT) consensus algorithm which was simpler and faster than the algorithms that had come before. So with all this history and momentum, why was the invention of blockchain so special?

Why blockchain?

Prior to blockchain, the world of consensus algorithms was stuck on the issue of identity. For a start, all the existing algorithms assumed you'd know the people you were planning on exchanging data with. Or at least their computers. So there was already a level of semi-trust in the set-up of your system. And, secondly, the algorithms required a complex series of message-passing between all participants before you could finally agree on any data. So the messaging complexity didn't scale in a 1:1 manner with adding new nodes, instead it grew exponentially.

Blockchain came and blew all of that out of the water. No more trusted set-up or foreknowledge of the other people on the network, no problems with adding thousands or millions of other participants. Now you could share a common record of transactions, of history, of the truth, between millions of participants, without having to trust anyone. Just the maths behind the software. And if anyone tried to lie or alter the evidence, the whole network would say 'no'.

The Cambrian explosion

Fast forward the next few years from Satoshi's release of the white paper in 2008, through to the first release of the bitcoin software in 2009, the first pizza bought for bitcoins in 2010, price parity with an ounce of gold in 2013, the release of ethereum in 2015, and then an increasingly overwhelming array of start-ups and scams with the initial coin offerings (ICOs) of 2017.

Blockchain has gone up and over Gartner's hype cycle faster than any other technology before it. From the revolutionary promises of global grassroots currencies grown from the ground up, free trade between rich and poor nations, restoring power to the people by removing all middlemen, blockchain has seen it all. It's been truly amazing to watch the variety of ideas people want to build once they have a shared, irrevocable source of truth.

Any descriptions of the state of blockchain today will already be out of date by the time you read this book, so I won't try. Just to say that the sector seems to be divided into four main categories of companies:

- **Ledger builders**: companies or groups building new distributed ledgers.

- **dApp builders**: distributed applications in which both the software and the data are stored and distributed according to a BFT consensus process between peers.

- **Service providers**: such as consultancies, marketing and specialised banking, providing services to companies in one of the first two categories.

- **Centralized systems**: custodial services such as cryptocurrency exchanges where you interact with the blockchain through a trusted party

Within the first category, there are a vast number of blockchains currently sitting comfortably alongside a smaller number of BFT systems built on the older consensus algorithms (R3's Corda and Hyperledger Sawtooth to name a couple). People divide these various BFT distributed ledger systems into categories such as public and private, trusted and trustless, but the distinctions aren't relevant here.

Many companies of the first two groups are in a period

of rapid experimentation trying to tackle complex multi-user and multi-party problems, and prove that distributing the system makes it more resilient against attacks and failures, improving the relationship between individuals and companies.

The topics being explored across the industry are incredibly broad and well matched to the times in which we live: improving sustainability of supply chains, better sharing of healthcare data, more responsive corporate management, better provision of local government services and even safer air traffic control.

The road from here

Ask yourself this: had you heard of byzantine faults, distributed systems or consensus before you encountered blockchain? For the vast majority of people, the answer will be no. These subjects were out there, being researched by small teams dotted around the world, but generally consigned to footnotes in computer science and certainly not making splashy headlines.

The near volcanic eruption of blockchain onto the world scene has taken the radical ideas of distribution, peer to peer and trust into places as diverse as banking, forestry and even space. Many of the early radicals in the blockchain world (early being an amusing term here because it was less than ten years ago) fell in love with the technology as a potential solution to many of the world's perceived ills: the excesses of capitalism, the increasing divide between the haves and have-nots, the forthcoming environmental catastrophe. These same people are still around, innovating and continuing to strive for transformation.

Blockchain can't be uninvented. The trust machine can't be stopped. But the ideas of iconoclasm and rebuilding the world without institutions or middlemen have been tempered somewhat by the experiences of the real world.

Instead I see the coming world of blockchain divided into two phases. The first will have more mature experimentation with ever larger groups of companies and even governments coming together to explore what canonical, irrefutable shared data means to their everyday operations. This will be followed by a vast dying off of unsustainable or unsuitable use cases for the technology, followed by a proliferation of trust machines behind the scenes in almost every aspect of our lives. One can only hope that these hold up to the original ideals of ensuring a better life for everyone.

Dr Robert Learney is head of distributed systems at Digital Catapult. He is involved in developing new programmes to help groups of companies from multiple sectors explore the potential of this technology to unlock economic growth for the United Kingdom. Prior to joining the Catapult, Rob co-founded the Imperial College Centre for Cryptocurrency Research and Engineering in 2014, aiming to create a cross-disciplinary academic focal point for blockchain research in London, and has been following developments across this sector ever since.

2.

A REVOLUTION
IN TRANSACTIONS

Thomas Hartmann and Elke Kunde at IBM highlight how four technical features of blockchain are combining to redefine how networks of partners and suppliers can now work together

Electronic distributed ledgers are still a fairly recent technology. They are revolutionizing the processing of transactions, especially in the form of blockchain, the most prominent member of this technology family, which is a shared, decentral and immutable register of transactions.

Shared

'Shared' in this context means that several parties agree to joint bookkeeping for assets of any kind, covering all and any changes in their state during a transaction. No one records their own representation of the transaction, exchanging point-to-point messages as it progresses.

Bilateral messaging works fairly well, as long as all parties are applying identical data and values. Any variation can cause confusion, leading to disputes about the correct, agreed values., which can be a time-consuming manual process to resolve.

A shared ledger creates one logical register where issuers of a transaction send it into the network to be validated against a set of jointly pre-defined rules by each relevant participant, depending on business logic and blockchain implementation.

These rules are specified in multiple layers. For example, the consensus method chosen by the network for validating transactions in general or as part of a process in a so-called smart contract, a piece of code on a blockchain that triggers a transaction or forwards it through the workflow.

Decentral

A blockchain is a shared but 'decentral' register, meaning each participant operates its own copy which is maintained by the consensus method and will have new blocks appended once transactions are validated. There is no central storing of the data and no single administration.

The validation of transactions is conducted independently by each participant based on the information in its own copy of the register. The result is communicated back to the consensus method in peer-to-peer mode: every participant can be a sender or a recipient of a transaction.

Immutable

Once a transaction has been put in a block and distributed it cannot be changed, inserted or deleted. Blocks can only be appended to the chain. So a blockchain is automatically building up the provenance of documents or an audit trail of transactions that can be traced back.

The 'immutability' of a blockchain is secured by hashes, ie, cryptographic checksums. Information about each transaction is stored with its respective hash. A hash is a standard function and each application can be programmed to create this kind of checksum. A hash is a one-way mathematical function and will, given the same input value, always deliver the same checksum that cannot be re-engineered to recreate the input value by backward calculation.

Once an application has computed the hash of a transaction, it can be compared with the stored hash in the blockchain to ensure the information is identical to its original value.

Blockchain implementations will build and finalize blocks of transactions at a defined pace. Some will use a fixed-time base; others are volume based; or a combination of the two might be used. Each new block will also store the hash value of its entire contents. The first information in a new block is the number and hash value of the previous one in the chain. In this way, an auditable system of values and checksums are interwoven among several blocks, thus assuring:

- Transaction values cannot be changed later, otherwise the block/transaction hash will not fit to the block/transaction value and the block hash is no longer correct.

- Blocks cannot be inserted, updated or deleted, as otherwise the block hash in the following block will not be correct anymore.

Finality

The result is 'finality'. As all relevant participants were involved in the validation of transactions, they will accept the results. Usually this result is also communicated to the register faster than in a non-shared ledger with overnight batch processing and subsequent messaging to the respective parties.

A blockchain is a distributed system, so consensus takes time. However, depending on the method for implementation and consensus, final and validated results can be available within seconds. This faster turnaround reduces the potential for fraud in the form of double spending due to incomplete or outdated information.

Different consensus methods not only affect performance and energy consumption, but also result in different finality models: firm finality at any fixed point in time; or eventual consistency where the blockchain might be exceptionally ambiguous in the form of a 'soft fork', where two versions of the ledger co-exist for some time until resolved.

Therefore, the choice of consensus model will be driven by the underlying business use case and its requirements for finality.

These four capabilities of a blockchain create trust in a multiparty network and are the technical foundation of a secure collaboration between enterprises, institutions and authorities.

Thomas Hartmann is an expert consultant with IBM Services, working as lead for blockchain in financial services for IBM Global Business Services in the DACH market (Germany, Austria and Switzerland). Thomas has over 25 years of experience in transforming the banking industry with a particular focus on payments and on back office operations in transaction banking at banks and market infrastructures. He got involved in blockchain in 2015 when the fit of the technology for enterprise use was taking its first important steps and is keen on keeping the focus where it adds tangible advantages to end users over 'conventionally digital' bank offerings.

Elke Kunde is an IT architect with IBM Germany's enterprise technical sales, acting as blockchain technical focal point for IBM in the DACH market (Germany, Austria, Switzerland). She is representing IBM

Germany as an expert in blockchain standardisation at the German DIN, as well as ISO/TC 30 (blockchain and electronic distributed ledger technologies) and Bitkom's blockchain working group. Elke has more than 20 years' experience in various roles in technical sales for IBM clients in banking, financial markets and insurance.

For further reading, see: *Blockchain for Dummies,* 3rd IBM Edition at https://www.ibm.com/downloads/cas/ OK5M0E49; *The Founder's Handbook* at https://www. ibm.com/downloads/cas/GZPPMWM5; and *Blockchain as a force for good* at https://www.ibm.com/downloads/ cas/AGL5ZWLN.

3.

BLOCKCHAIN, CYBERPUNKS AND FINANCIAL INNOVATION

Blockchain technology might have been the creation of cyberpunks, but it is fast joining the financial mainstream, reports Jonny Fry at Team Blockchain

Blockchain technology and the digital assets it creates now represent more than just potential. Globally, they are actually transforming governments, industries and even people's behaviour. While blockchain has been around since the 1970s, it was broadly unknown, apart from academic circles, until 2008 following the financial turbulence that resulted in the collapse of Lehman Brothers and the creation of bitcoin.

Bitcoin harnessed blockchain to facilitate 'trusted interactions over the internet', thus enabling strangers worldwide to buy and sell from each other in an anonymous fashion without using banks or indeed any other financial institution. Unfortunately, this gave rise to those involved in nefarious activities, such as money laundering, arms dealing, drug barons and human trafficking, among the early adopters and users. Websites such as The Silk Road, where you could buy guns, narcotics and even assassins, flourished with transactions using untraceable bitcoins as the currency of choice. When the FBI finally closed The Silk Road in October 2013, it became one of the largest holders of bitcoin.

In simplistic terms, blockchain enables:

- Creation of a data base: a spreadsheet with military-grade security with copies of the data held in multiple locations.

- Transfer of value without double counting.

- Digital footprints: an immutable record of transactions and information.

- Transparency, provenance and traceability.

- Risk mitigation: programmes in compliance and regulation.

Together, these qualities lead to greater trust, a rare commodity in a world bombarded with fake news and have inspired tech start-ups everywhere to tackle projects in almost every industry, as well as charitable endeavours, such as the initiative from SC Johnson and Plastic Bank that has led to the recycling of 8000 tons of plastic. The requirement of many of these ventures for capital led to the creation of what become known as initial coin offerings (ICOs).

ICOs

In 2014, Mastercoin launched the first ICO, but it took nearly three years for ICOs to really take off, resulting in the issue of over 5500 tokens and raising over $30 billion on a global basis. It was not just start-ups that launched ICOs. In Germany, Naga was the first quoted European firm to launch one, raising over €40 million from 63,000 subscribers. It was particularly interesting as, historically, German investors tend to be cautious and this ICO was based in Belize.

However, the problem was that ICOs were largely unregulated, so leading to a number of questionable operators and outright scams. It has been claimed that up to 80 percent of all ICOs are scams, which seems harsh, but no doubt many were highly questionable. Although many ICOs have struggled to survive unfortunately, it has not been all doom and gloom.

For example, according to Ripple, the World Bank calculates that $1.6 trillion of costs are incurred as money is moved from one bank to another globally. Ripple claims it can do this job faster and cheaper than the current system, Swift. Whilst Santander is the only bank that owns equity in Ripple, over a hundred international banks are now conducting trials which may explain why Ripple's value rose by over 35,000 percent during 2017. No wonder ICOs caught investors' imagination.

As regulators turned their attention to ICOs and argued that many of them should be treated as securities, it has led to the development of STOs (security token offerings). STOs are normally backed by an asset and are typically subject to security regulations in the jurisdiction in which they are marketed and launched. The type of assets to which they are linked include private and publicly traded shares and bonds, property (both residential and commercial), commodities such as gold and diamonds and intellectual property. The potential list goes on. STOs, being digital assets, mean that potentially they can be listed on regulated digital exchanges which, in theory, enables them to be traded 24/7 allowing smaller investors access to buy and sell these assets.

Digital currencies

Business leaders are now commenting on the impact that blockchain and digital assets are beginning to have:

- 'What the internet did for communications, I think blockchain will do for trusted transactions', Ginni Rometty, IBM's former chief executive.

- 'Bitcoin is a remarkable cryptographic achievement and the ability to create something that is not duplicable in the digital world has enormous value', Eric Schmidt, chief executive, Google.

- 'Your kids won't know what (paper) money is', Tim Cook, chief executive, Apple.

Following Tim Cook's comment, we have seen Facebook announce that it's hankering to launch its own digital currency, Libra, thus creating a medium of exchange for its 2.3 billion customers, potentially bypassing the banks. While it has not had a universally positive response, Mark Carney, former governor of the Bank of England, proposed at a meeting of the US Federal Reserve that the days of the dollar as the world's reserve currency may be numbered. However, rather than being replaced by another fiat currency, such as the Chinese renminbi, a digital currency like Facebook's Libra might be the alternative.

While it has not been universally popular, it was interesting to observe in May 2020 that Stuart Levey, the ex-head of HSBC Legal, is to head up Libra as its chief executive. Given that Levey was under-secretary for terrorism and financial intelligence at the US Treasury for seven years, he will be well aware of what is acceptable to governments and financial institutions.

Indeed, in 2019 Christian Legarde, former managing director of the International Monetary Fund, said in a speech in Singapore:

> A new wind is blowing, that of digitalization. In this new world, we meet anywhere, any time. The town square is back — virtually, on our smartphones. We exchange information,

services, even emojis, instantly, peer to peer, person to person. We float through a world of information, where data is the new gold, despite growing concerns over privacy and cybersecurity. A world in which millennials are reinventing how our economy works, phone in hand.

Meanwhile in China, the People's Bank of China (PBOC), has the dual mandate of maintaining price stability whilst promoting growth by using a selection of monetary policies. One of the ways that the PBOC is hoping it can assert greater control over its economy is by launching its own digital currency. The crux of the proposal is to initially replace only cash with a digital currency, not bank deposits.

It is intended that the digital currency will offer 'controllable privacy': like cash, payments can be made without handing over personal details, which are 'loosely coupled' with an account. The PBOC will be able to view transactions, helping to minimize the risk of tax evasion and other illegal activities within China. The introduction of a digital currency will extend the government's influence and control, as was outlined by its vice-governor, Fan Yifei: 'There will be variable transaction fees, as well as daily and annual transaction limits, to give the central bank more tools to control the velocity of money and its supply when interest rates cease to be a viable channel for intervention'.

It is also hoped that a digital currency, backed by the PBOC and with the same legal status as a banknote, will lower the cost of financial transactions thereby helping to make financial services more widely available. This could be especially significant in China where millions of people are still 'unbanked'. A digital currency should also be cheaper to operate and is anticipated it will reduce fraud and counterfeiting.

China will be initially launching its digital currency in five cities and the government is proposing to use it to pay some of its employees 50 percent of their May 2020 transportation subsidies. Furthermore, McDonald's, Starbucks and Subway are all reported to have agreed to accept it, alongside Tencent, Ant Financial and four state-owned banks as part of a roll-out to retail and catering.

The Chinese are likely to embrace their new digital currency readily as, according to McKinsey, mobile payments have been eleven times the value of those in the United States since 2017. Indeed, McKinsey reports that China now accounts for 40 percent of global e-commerce transactions, up from 1 percent just a few years ago.

Financial services

In financial services, we are also seeing blockchain being used to help to lower costs and remove some of the third parties currently involved in issuing bonds. The World Bank (in conjunction with Commonwealth Bank of Australia, Royal Bank of Canada and TD Securities) has, for the second time in a year, used blockchain to raise $33 million in bonds, taking the total it has now raised to over $100 million so far.

Sophie Gilder, head of blockchain at Commonwealth Bank of Australia was reported as saying: 'CBA now has tangible evidence ... that blockchain can deliver a new level of efficiency, transparency, and risk-management capability versus the existing market infrastructure. Next we intend to deliver additional functionality to deliver greater efficiencies in settlement, custody and regulatory compliance'.

According to Thomson Reuters, there was over $6.6 trillion of debt issued globally in 2018. If the costs of issuing bonds could be reduced by just 20 percent (some firms claim it could be a lot more) then potentially the savings could be in the order of $660 million a year. Little wonder there is more and more interest in using blockchain to eliminate the layers of costs and intermediaries, not to mention the greater transparency and risk controls that can be implemented.

As well as the cost savings that blockchain offers, it also potentially enables smaller tranches of bonds to be issued by SMEs, opening up a new source of capital for them. These smaller bond offerings could challenge the peer-to-peer lending markets that have proved so successful in the last few years.

Blockchain is also being used in the asset management industry via the tokenization of funds which, in Deloitte's view, 'allows the creation of a new financial system, one that is more democratic, more efficient and faster than anything we have seen'.

Tokenization of an existing fund makes it more appealing to younger investors, who are increasingly looking to buy and sell funds digitally on mobile devices (without the need for face-to-face financial advice). Tokenization can create more transparency by building in automated compliance and lower transactions costs, thus giving asset managers a powerful incentive to adopt it.

Ironically, it was concern over the dark web and the anonymity of transactions (by using bitcoin) that made the regulators suspicious of blockchain initially. However, we could now well see this technology being actively encouraged by these same sceptics. As the *Financial Times* asked: 'could a progressive regulator mandate a wholesale move to blockchain?'

Agriculture embraces blockchain

It is not solely in financial services where blockchain is being embraced. In agriculture, blockchain-powered platforms are being built to make the tracking and provenance of food easier, whilst improving the efficiency of supply chains.

In Brazil, coffee farmers will soon have access to a cryptocurrency called 'coffeecoin'. According to a report on Bloomberg, coffeecoin is being launched by one of Brazil's biggest arabica-coffee co-operatives, Minasul. It will enable farmers to buy machinery and fertilizer, as well as non-farm products such as cars and food. Coffeecoin is part of Minasul's strategy to encourage farmers to embrace new technology. As a result, the farmers will be able to sell coffee beans via a mobile phone, thus cutting out unnecessary intermediaries and improving price transparency.

Coffee beans are the second most-traded commodity

globally after crude oil with an estimated market of $100 billion. The introduction of a cryptocurrency in the world's largest producer, Brazil, will be followed closely by competitors, such as Vietnam and Colombia, looking for gains in efficiency and improvements for farmers.

Already the use of blockchain in agriculture and food supply is estimated to be $61 million, according to ReportLinker, and is projected to grow 47 percent a year to reach $429 million by 2025. This growth is being driven by customers demanding greater transparency about the source of their food, how sustainable it is and the environmental impacts of what they are consuming.

In the US, large tech firms, such as IBM and Microsoft, and international retailers and food processors, such as Walmart, McCormick and Dole Food Company, are all driving the use of blockchain in agriculture. If coffeecoin is a success, other commodity producers will probably look to create their own version (such as wheatcoin, corncoin or tobaccocoin) which, provided there is sufficient liquidity, could then offer an alternative way for traders and investors to get exposure to these commodities.

Conclusion

The adoption of blockchain and digital assets was initially driven bottom-up: cyberpunks who wanted to bypass banks, such as those engaged in dodgy deals on The Silk Road. It was also used by small tech start-ups which, via ICOs, issued cryptocurrencies as a way to raise capital. Increasingly, we are seeing more top-down advocates: governments and multinational corporates, such as Goldman Sachs, Allianz, SC Johnson and Facebook, implementing blockchain to solve real commercial and environmental challenges.

There is still a need for better infrastructure for trading digital assets and clearer guidance from regulators. There is also the question of whether quantum computers will be able to hack into the military-grade security that blockchain currently uses. Finally, there is the added challenge of keeping up to date as the blockchain and digital assets sectors are developing so quickly. One of the main factors holding back their greater use is a lack of education and knowledge about what is possible.

Jonny Fry is co-founder and chief executive of Team Blockchain, a blockchain, crypto, digital assets and funds specialist. He has over 25 years' experience as chief executive of a UK-regulated asset management company which he floated on the London Stock Exchange. Through his focus on the dynamics of financial innovation, he now advises on how blockchain technology and digital assets are being used in the commercial world. Jonny writes a widely distributed weekly analysis, *Digital Bytes*, reporting on the development and growth of blockchain technology and digital assets, highlighting examples of how, where and why they are being used. To receive Digital Bytes please register using this link:

http://eepurl.com/gTDiwP. Jonny is also non-executive chairman of Gemini Investment Management Ltd and co-founder of the British Blockchain Frontier Technology Association (BBFTA).

4.

BLOCKCHAIN AND THE
TRANSFORMATION OF BANKING

Digital identity, lower payment costs and open offerings of debt or equity add up to a powerful stimulus to growth, says Sean Kiernan at DAG Global, a pioneer digital merchant bank

Blockchain, or distributed ledger technology (DLT), is now finally being seen as a distinct technology from the cryptocurrencies that brought it to our attention. It is increasingly recognized as the path towards delivering a new industrial revolution, providing a means of trusted communication and exchange that can be publicly verified and, ultimately, strengthening mechanisms of trust. The logic behind blockchain is potentially as revolutionary for the future as the internet that made it possible. Much work, much investment, is now going into establishing transformational use cases for blockchain's deployment, not only in already mature and sophisticated areas like financial services, but in any sector where information needs to be stored or transferred. These now include healthcare, real estate, asset ownership, but more are emerging by the day. According to Gartner, a leading technology research and advisory company, 'by 2030, the business value added by blockchain will grow to $3.1 trillion'.

The United Kingdom, with its inherent strengths in finance and technology, is therefore well placed to take a leading position in building this innovation economy, according to *Blockchain Industry Landscape Overview*, a report[1] published by DAG with the UK's All-Party Parliamentary Group on Blockchain, together with established thought leaders including The Big Innovation Centre and Deep Knowledge Ventures. The report outlines the current state of blockchain investment in the UK as well as the considerable ecosystem that has emerged. No less than 225 blockchain companies across a variety of sectors have been identified and explained. All this has been achieved largely without a supportive UK industrial strategy, in contrast to the likes of Malta which has made a significant effort to court the sector.

Yet in the UK, many existing banks will not service blockchain businesses (let alone anything connected to cryptocurrency), citing fears of reputational or regulatory risk in facilitating money laundering. These fears are by no means baseless, although recent developments in what has been termed as blockchain analysis can enable every transaction on reputable public blockchains to be tracked, so that flows can be clearly sourced right back to their origin.

Checking flows in blockchain-based digital instruments is already more robust when compared to traditional fiat currency-based transactions, where often it is only possible to trace sources of funds to the immediately prior institution in what is always a longer chain. The UK Treasury Select Committee's September 2018 comprehensive report[2] on cryptoassets, spoke of 'regulation needed for Wild West cryptoasset market'. The report was 'tentatively positive' on such novel blockchain-based instruments, but work remains to be done to develop regulatory frameworks and standards of governance so that general acceptance can follow. This work has been furthered by the Financial Conduct Authority's cryptoasset taskforce, as well as recently by the FCA's consultation paper published in October 2019, *Recovery of costs of supervising cryptoasset businesses under the proposed anti-money laundering regulations: fees proposals.*

A Bank of England report[3] in July 2016 estimated that the UK's GDP could increase by 3 percent just by introducing a Central Bank Digital Currency (CBDC). Our own comprehensive analysis[4] of the UK's blockchain economy after Brexit, published in 2019 with GMEX, a technology services company also operating in the blockchain space, confirms these figures. We show that a digital economy is a positive counter measure to the claimed negative economic impact of Brexit (on the Bank of England's own account) by promising the same percentage growth (3 percent) that is being predicted as a contraction. Establishing a digital economy, in other words, has the power to erase the negative effect of Brexit entirely. Potentially even, with clear vision and a bit more derring-do, why should the impacts of Brexit be negative at all?

Against this backdrop, DAG Global seeks to be the UK's first digital merchant bank. As we see it, the challenge is to bring traditional merchant banking disciplines back into practice by using digital means to enable cost-effective and client-focused services. We are excited by the potential of blockchain to transform financial services. Many use cases are being explored, although we see its influence taking shape in three particular areas.

Digital identity

Each financial services company currently conducts standalone KYC (know your customer) and AML (anti-money laundering) checks on their clients, before onboarding them with new accounts or before facilitating their transactions. With the advent of GDPR and open banking, and with increased focus on individual clients owning their data, several initiatives are under development that aim to offer clients a digital passport on the blockchain that allows them to store securely their own data in a way that they can grant access to financial institutions to onboard them with a consistent process. In effect, it shifts the emphasis from individual financial services firms conducting standalone KYC to a collaborative effort where if a client is *bona fide* they can agree to share details of their digital passport and thus directly obtain access to financial services. This development has enormous potential to open up access and increase financial inclusion, and also rewire the costs of compliance to a centralized approach which should ultimately reduce costs for switching accounts or engaging in transactions with an aim to empower the consumer with additional choice.

Plummeting payments transaction costs

Most Western economies are deploying the same legacy infrastructure for payments transactions as has been in place for decades. This has allowed for a highly robust system that can withstand shocks in the system, given trusted mechanisms and established recognized procedures, but it also has resulted in a relatively high cost and a lengthy procedure for making payments, particularly overseas.

On the other hand, innovative companies operating in China, such as Alibaba's AliPay and Tencent's WeChat Pay, have taken a completely different approach to payments, and have deployed a fully digital back end which allows for instantaneous and nearly free payments between users within the respective company payment ecosystems. This approach is similar to what Facebook is looking to deploy with its Libra cryptocurrency. We expect the rise of CBDCs (central bank digital currencies) and similar projects, including Ripple, to gradually digitize the rails of international payments and transform this sector as well.

Digital debt and equity offerings

There have been considerable efforts and advances in exploring DeFi or decentralized finance as a mechanism to democratize access to financial products. The rise of crowdfunding and crowdlending platforms, for example, has opened access for retail investors to participate in equity or debt offerings that had been previously only been available for institutional investors. This presents both opportunities and risks, particularly for those retail investors who may not have suitable risk profiles to engage in such instruments.

We are firm believers in open capital markets as a means for economies and investors to efficiently allocate capital to growing companies and industries.

One area of the economy that has struggled to gain access to the capital markets has been SMEs, given the inherent costs of structuring traditional bonds and conducting initial public offerings on the equity markets. The rise of more cost-effective digital debt and equity offerings, as structured on the blockchain, should also be transformational in opening up the promise of crowdfunding to a new asset class and in removing barriers to entry for these firms to raise capital. Promising efforts to open this new area have been launched by the SIX Digital Exchange in Switzerland, for example, as well as several other efforts in the US, UK and elsewhere to offer platforms to provide custody and exchange services for digital security tokens.

The global blockchain and digital assets sector is undergoing widespread integration in the technology and financial ecosystem, however digital asset companies struggle to find access to mainstream banking services. This has given rise to a significant gap in its core markets such as the US and the UK. Digital asset companies seeking to pave the way for blockchain-based financial services have flourished, but still face challenges with access to traditional banking services, products and liquidity being one of the most pressing. Thus far, no institution in the UK has stepped in to bridge the significant gap in demand; DAG will be the first UK bank to focus on this space. A similar problem exists for SMEs, who have difficulty accessing funding from high street banks, as well as challenger or non-bank lenders who do not have the scale to service the whole market. We intend to be part of an exciting story that is unfolding rapidly in the transformation of financial services.

Sean Kiernan is chief executive and founder of DAG Global, the UK's first digital asset merchant bank, whose focus is purely on SMEs. It is currently applying for regulatory permissions to deliver next-generation merchant banking solutions, including deposit-taking and lending, to blockchain and digital asset companies, SMEs and fintech companies, which are being underserved by existing banks and non-bank lenders. DAG is set up to offer fiat and digital products and services to practice standards of compliance and security with enhanced due diligence. Further details at: www.dag.global.

Notes

1. *Blockchain in UK: Blockchain industry landscape overview 2018*, DAG Global, Big Innovation Centre and Deep Knowledge Analytics in co-ordination with the All Party Parliamentary Group on Blockchain: https://www.dkv.global/blockchain-in- uk

2. *Cryptoassets*, a report of the House of Commons Treasury Select Committee, September 2018: https://publications.parliament.uk/pa/cm201719/cmselect/cmtreasy/910/91002.htm

3. *The macroeconomics of central bank issued cryptocurrencies*, Bank of England, staff working 605, July 2016: https://www.bankofengland.co.uk/-/media/boe/files/working-paper/2016/the-macroeconomics-of-central-bank-issued-digital-currencies.pdf?la=en&hash=341B602838707E5D6FC26884588C912A721B1DC1

4. *The Digital Opportunity of Brexit: A blockchain economy in the UK*, a report by GMEX Group and Dag Global, December 2018: https://www.gmex-group.com/article-the-digital-opportunity-of-brexit-a-blockchain-economy-in-the-uk/

5.

BLOCKCHAIN ADOPTION
IN BUSINESS

Thomas Hartman and Elke Kunde at IBM trace the dynamic development of blockchain applications in business

Blockchain technology has advanced since the first practical application in the well-known cryptocurrency bitcoin about ten years ago. Bitcoin's original use was anarchic in inspiration: the inventor wanted to send money in a secure way from sender A to recipient B without having banks involved and without giving authorities, or in fact any third party, the option of stopping the transaction. To accomplish this, all participants in the network are anonymous with access to transactions with their respective cryptographic keys.

Proof of work

A consensus method called proof of work (PoW) enables secure processing of transactions that prevents tampering in an anonymous environment. In this consensus method, network participants are randomly chosen to build new blocks for the network. To protect the networks from anyone manipulating the block, a competition is part of the consensus method: the blocks contain a cryptographic checksum which is incomplete. It is however not possible to simply compute the result of this puzzle; the correct checksum has to be found in a trial-and-error approach.

This operation which is needed for each new block is computing intensive and processed by multiple and, in some networks, competing parties. As a result, blockchain technology has gained the somewhat general reputation of requiring enormous computing power resulting in immense energy consumption, questioning the efficiency of the technology overall.

Miners

The first of the competing parties to determine the correct checksum for the new block broadcasts the result to the network for others to validate. As an incentive for being the first, they are awarded a fraction of cryptocurrency newly created at this instance. Those who finalize blocks in a PoW consensus have come to be known as miners.

As this trial-and-error approach is a competition, large

miners with vast computing power have no guarantee of winning. The concept is considered being safe, as long as malicious or fraudulent miners are not able to get a 51 percent majority of computing power in the network.

From cryptocurrencies to smart contracts

The first blockchain implementations were dedicated to payment use cases, thus all of them have a built-in cryptocurrency. As a currency is traditionally being issued by an authority like a central bank, the more neutral term of 'digital asset' might be more appropriate. Discussions are continuing to this day.

A lot of pilot and research projects broadened the landscape of blockchain technology in the past ten years, leading to implementations for different purposes with new capabilities. A lot of them have been developed in an open source approach as a group; others have been developed in private enterprises and institutions.

Smart contracts are among key capabilities for almost every blockchain implementation today, a feature that was missing in the original bitcoin design. A smart contract is a piece of code stored in a blockchain that processes results in the shared ledger. It translates business rules for transaction processing into code and if-then rules in ways that are highly deterministic and cannot be changed or skipped. Ethereum, an open source project, became the first to develop a working model.

While this functionality is extremely useful and

popular, the term can still cause confusion in thinking that this piece of code deals with contracts in a legal sense. While the exact legal nature of a smart contract is still under much debate, there have been other terms suggested for this functionality such as 'chaincode', as used by the Hyperledger Fabric community. As yet, none of the other alternative designations are being as broadly accepted in public discussion

The potential of this construct, however you term it, is huge: it provides customizable conditional transaction processing and the automation of workflows on a shared register that is immutable and secure, enabling transparent digital processes in a multi-party environment.

Initial uncertainties

Blockchain adoption in enterprises was slow in the first years for several reasons. The first implementations had anonymous or pseudonymous participants in a permissionless or public network, built-in own currencies and a slow consensus method in the form of PoW, not allowing the high transaction rates that business expects. An open register accessible and readable for everybody combined with a lack of clarity on governance and liabilities only reinforced the reservations. There was a need to build blockchain technology capable of fully reflecting today's requirements in business, including full compliance with existing laws and regulations.

Private blockchains

The idea of having a shared ledger was, and is, compelling for many enterprises, but it had to be done and operated in a different way. One of the next steps was the development of a shared ledger for a dedicated business network, a private permissioned blockchain. Participants must be able to know who they are dealing with.

Permissions are required to provide visibility of business data on a need-to-know basis and identities are key for implementing this functionality. Transactions are thus authenticated and verifiable, adding more security and trust into a digital workflow. Permissioned blockchains with a certificate authority run by a trusted agency issuing identities are a requirement for business networks.

Automation in a secure shared ledger enabled by smart contracts was also key, providing business terms and rules in code to execute transactions. The consensus method must be able to scale and enable performant transaction processing at enterprise level.

Such use of identities in a blockchain network also enables more efficient consensus methods than proof of work. Quorum decisions or role-based decisions are possible when using identity-based consensus, some of them are even resistant to fraudulent participants. As different use cases may need different consensus methods, it is a good idea to enable configurable consensus methods for the respective business networks, each choosing the method best suited to their needs.

There are several blockchain implementations that implement these requirements entirely or to a large extent. The creation of a secure register for adoption by a larger number of users depends on a co-ordinated collaborative approach.

Hyperledger, of which IBM is a founding member, is an open source project for building blockchains for business hosted by the Linux Foundation. For a secure register, other parties have to be able to inspect the code's base, which is why open source matters. A collaborative approach with an open but clear structure of governance leads to a broad contribution and adoption of the technology.

At the foundation of Hyperledger in 2016, IBM donated its own former own implementation to the project. IBM still is a major contributor to Hyperledger Fabric, the first of the six blockchain frameworks currently being hosted by Hyperledger project. Hyperledger Fabric is the base technology of IBM's blockchain platform and many blockchain solutions for business.

Blockchain for business is adopting the ideas behind bitcoin, integrating prior research on distributed computing. A variety of solutions are being deployed to suit circumstances in different industries. As a result, one of the rising key challenges of this environment is ensuring the interoperability between these business blockchains. Blockchain technology is developing dynamically, already opening up novel efficiencies with many more to follow.

Thomas Hartmann is an expert consultant with IBM Services, working as lead for blockchain in financial services for IBM Global Business Services in the DACH market (Germany, Austria and Switzerland). Thomas has over 25 years of experience in transforming the banking industry with a particular focus on payments and on back office operations in transaction banking at banks and market infrastructures. He got involved in blockchain in 2015 when the fit of the technology for enterprise use was taking its first important steps and is keen on keeping the focus where it adds tangible advantages to end users over 'conventionally digital' bank offerings.

Elke Kunde is an IT architect with IBM Germany's enterprise technical sales, acting as blockchain technical focal point for IBM in the DACH market (Germany, Austria, Switzerland). She is representing IBM Germany as an expert in blockchain standardisation at the German DIN, as well as ISO/TC 30 (blockchain and electronic distributed ledger technologies) and Bitkom's blockchain working group. Elke has more than 20 years' experience in various roles in technical sales for IBM clients in banking, financial markets and insurance.

For further reading, see: *Blockchain for Dummies,* 3rd IBM Edition at https://www.ibm.com/downloads/cas/

OK5M0E49; *The Founder's Handbook* at https://www.
ibm.com/downloads/cas/GZPPMWM5; and *Blockchain
as a force for good* at https://www.ibm.com/downloads/
cas/AGL5ZWLN.

6.

VALUE CREATION WITH BLOCKCHAIN

Data sharing in a trust economy is leading to a series of transformative impacts, reports Chris Painter at Omnitude

Bitcoin is the poster child of blockchain, It has carried its standard for its entire, but brief history. Blockchain has traditionally found itself associated with cryptocurrency, but the broader technological benefits are probably best understood when you take a step back from this singular use case.

If you replace the principle of the transaction of currency via a distributed network and ledger, and remove the mining component, you are still left with a hugely advantageous system to securely, transparently and immutably transact value. It is this term, value, that will become hugely powerful to both businesses and individuals in the future.

When you understand what this value could represent,

you can start to build a picture of where blockchain can add commercial advantage. So what is valuable in today's ultra-connected society?

Data

Often described as 'the new oil', data has recently been in the spotlight both from a corporate governance and an individual standpoint. With recent scandals around data leaks from Facebook, and individual concerns about online identity and privacy, the increased security and the immutable nature that blockchain offers can start to address these issues on a granular level.

A self-sovereign identity

From an individual standpoint, blockchain and distributed ledger technology, once combined with control interfaces, allows individuals a secure and manageable way to own their digital identities and data. They can control who sees what data via a series of permissions, even seeking to earn rewards for sharing that data directly with companies that they trust. With the ability to reward via cryptocurrency-based transactions, it affords the opportunity for entirely new interactions directly between brands and consumers that have up until now always had to go through a middleman.

In the future, it may well mean that businesses and brands that put their customers' needs at the heart of their operations gain a greater data advantage than those that choose to ignore the needs and wants of their customer base. Through small micro-transactions, organizations can start to create an increasingly clearer picture of their customer demographic that is infinitely more accurate and detailed than has ever previously been possible. As legislation around the sharing of data, such as GDPR, becomes increasingly tighter, the ability of organizations to purchase generic data from brokers will reduce. By earning data instead, important decisions around stock control, demand and opportunities for growth will go to the business that can adopt this new paradigm.

The trust economy

For example, if James buys jeans from an online retailer two times a year, but actually buys cargo pants three times a year from another completely different retailer online, it is a customer behaviour that will never be understood by the jeans retailer. Now if there is a positive relationship between James and the jeans retailer, if asked, James may well (for a small reward) allow the jeans retailer access to this aspect of his data set. This could then allow the jeans retailer an insight that they might well have never had access to.

One James doesn't sound like a business-defining insight, but if it becomes 100,000 Jameses, then that business may well have enough information to make a judgement call on whether they should actually be selling cargo pants as well.

This advantage can be gained only through the

application of a secure blockchain platform, which secures identity, gives the consumer granular control and bakes in an inherent reward system. For the retailer too, blockchain makes a difference: it allows the establishment of trust between themselves and James, but also it can prove that James' identity is genuine and that the data supplied can be trusted. These are the new types of loyalty and B2C relationships that can be established when you are working within a blockchain enabled trust economy.

Identity systems

Identity doesn't just stop at individuals. It can be applied to many aspects of our digital world. A self-sovereign identity system split into three distinct areas, working across:

- individuals enabling a new privacy in our digital world;

- organizations, allowing data sharing on a permissioned basis and the automation of tasks between actors;

- devices, allowing safety and compliance across any device within the value chain, allowing status monitoring and automation.

Linking these systems of identity up seamlessly via a middleware platform allows a plug-and-play solution for any individual or business wanting to leverage the benefits of blockchain in its current systems.

Supply chains

For business, there are many more examples where instances of shared and trusted data can bring advantages. Today global supply chains have become intricate, complex and sometimes opaque. Where materials and components for manufacture are amalgamated from a broad range of sources, there arise many questions about authenticity and provenance.

If all parties and actors within these chains are able to reference an immutable record of trust, then the advantages start to become apparent. Long-winded processes of receipt and certification can be automated via smart contracts (a computer protocol designed to automatically facilitate, enforce and complete a contract between participants without the need for third parties). Improvements in security and efficiency mean that supply chains are one of the most fertile industries for the application of this new technology. With the ability to combat fraud and counterfeiting of goods, provide safety certification, and confirm provenance and sustainability, blockchain is positioned to transform this sector in fundamental ways.

Proof of origin for consumers

Businesses that can prove the provenance of their goods and services on the blockchain will have a competitive advantage over those that don't, especially in a world where individuals are becoming more and more concerned about such matters. Until recently the baby boomers and Generation X have been less demanding about the origination and sustainability of the goods and services they buy.

Increasingly we are seeing a shift in this attitude towards a more responsible stance in purchasing behaviour with millennials onwards, putting these concerns at the top of their decision tree. Any business that can harness the immutable proof of origin that blockchain can provide will find it has an edge over those businesses that can't.

Generally, there is a real opportunity for brands and consumers to start to be able to demonstrate this technology through digital proof via QR codes etc. At the point of purchase or on products, businesses and brands via blockchain can deliver the product or service story through smart phone interaction and augmented messaging. Will the end user every really need to know it is blockchain? Maybe not, but as awareness of this technology grows, so will user demand that proof be supplied.

Life sciences

The advantages that blockchain brings to life sciences opens up the potential for huge market disruption in a sector that depends on the efficacy of data and service delivery in life-critical situations. The security across distributed networks of data can be harnessed to radically improve performance and disrupt operating models.

Trust protocols, for instance, are now being introduced to clinical drug trials with a view to gaining more patient-positive outcomes. It is paramount within the process that the data received is trusted. All of the complex interaction points within the process are monitored and measured, ensuring data is correctly received, processed and stored in a manner that creates trust in the results.

Blockchain's immutable proof of interaction can be stored within a single longitudinal record within the network from patient to provider, including all of the touchpoints in between. Patient data can be held within a self-sovereign identity and released on a permissioned basis to the organizations involved. With inclusion of the full spectrum of manufacturers, providers, clinicians, insurers, and patients within this trust network through a series of monitoring applications via smart devices, it not only allows historical accuracy in the results, but it also enables real-time monitoring of patient data.

The ability to enable this kind of interaction through middleware systems, connecting the broad range of participants and protecting that data in the blockchain speeds up process, highlights data concerns, and delivers an agreed final version of the results.

Add to this the ability for patients to own their own medical records, and, through permissioned access, allow that data to be shared across different institutions rather than storing it centrally, blockchain creates a much more efficient way of collation and cross-reference, giving individuals the chance to get accurate second opinions or share data with clinical specialists that will ultimately create more positive outcomes.

Conclusion

As the much-heralded fourth industrial revolution takes hold and artificial intelligence, machine learning and the internet of things start to transform the way individuals and organizations interact and operate with each other, the secure transmission, sharing and storing of data, becomes increasingly important. Blockchain, although the least glamourous and visible of these emerging technologies, could well be one of the most important aspects of the development of new opportunities within these fields.

The more we automate our lives and allow digital transformation, the more important trust becomes in ensuring that these new opportunities are enabled for the benefit of individuals and organizations alike.

Chris Painter has worked in digital development for 15 years. His technical background has been focused round the thorny issues of system integrations from day one, building software platforms that create links between disparate CRM, ERP and WMS legacy systems. He started Omnitude in November 2017 as a blockchain integration platform, with the vision of creating a mainstream channel for businesses to seek the advantages of DLT technology whilst minimising the pain of new technology integrations. He is a straight-talking, down-to-earth advocate of blockchain and its transformational potential within the real world.

7.

BLOCKCHAIN, FASHION AND DISRUPTIVE START-UPS

Blockchain is changing the rules for how fashion operates. Kevin R Smith reviews the impact made by two disruptive start-ups, A Transparent Company and BEEN London

Adapting to change is crucial for any company at any stage of its life, and innovation is key to adapting. True innovation comes from the creation of new technologies and ideas, as well as the use of those new technologies in disruptive ways. Just as necessity is the mother of invention, then it is the application of those inventions and advances that make the real difference.

Many innovations or advances enable certain industries or processes to make major strides forward, but seldom does the world benefit from an advance that has such wide-reaching and all-encompassing disruptive potential that it ultimately affects the lives of everyone. One such advance was the internal combustion engine and another was the internet. Both of these were originally seen by many to have limited potential, but history had other ideas.

And so it has been with blockchain. Whilst devotees of blockchain are the first to stress that blockchain is not the silver bullet that cures all problems and that adoptees should start with the problem and then realize that blockchain is the best answer, there is, nevertheless, a growing recognition by all areas of business that the use of blockchain does indeed solve many previously unsolvable problems. Indeed, blockchain is already touching most people's lives in many ways, whether they realize it or not.

Disruption and making swift decisions is not something that comes easily to the majority of larger corporates, but it is exactly the domain of start-ups. It is companies at this end of the market that are the true disruptors and pioneers, enabling larger corporates and whole industries to follow.

Whilst blockchain is being adopted in ever increasing ways, one of the areas in which it has already proven its worth on a global basis is in supply chains.

The fashion sector

The fashion sector is a $3 trillion dollar industry that is far from transparent and has fragmented and trustless supply chains. Historically, it has been difficult to track and trace materials from origin to end product in a way that keeps every actor in the supply chain accountable or for a brand to prove certain claims.

In many cases the raw materials or the manufacturing processes are far from being ethical or ecological, or indeed sustainable, in the longer term. Until relatively recently, consumers were either ill informed of the true underlying cost of the products that they bought and/or they simply did not care as long as they were able to buy what they wanted at the cheapest possible price.

But the world has now changed and many consumers care, and care passionately, about all aspects of the human and environmental impact of what they are buying. We have seen this change already in a move towards things such as free-range chickens, organic vegetables and, more recently, electric cars. But until now there has not been much change in the fashion industry due to its fragmented nature and low-tech, long supply chains.

Fortunately, the landscape is now changing from one that ignores the problem to one that is seeking answers. Many fashion manufacturers are now being asked to prove that their entire supply chain meets the ethical and environmental standards that are being demanded by consumers.

The first steps in using blockchain to solve this issue were a collaborative effort lead by start-up called A Transparent Company in May 2017. The process included utilizing blockchain-based software to track and trace in real time from farm to finished garment. Each step of the process was registered and tracked on the ethereum blockchain. Each garment had a unique smart label, enabling the designer to verify every step of its production and create a digital history of that information including location data, content and timestamps, all of which was presented to consumers via an interface they could access through their item's QR code or near field communication tag.

This pilot was a world first use case for the fashion industry, being a point of reference for the intersection between fashion, sustainability and blockchain. Its impact has travelled around the world, becoming a case study for education and business conferences, and inspiring others to adopt the practices that this proof of concept has pioneered — transparency in fashion.

Innovation is not a solution until it is scalable, and it was a start-up that has shown the way and encouraged large fashion manufacturers and brands to follow. The fashion industry has now started on this journey of transparency, and it is under ever-growing pressure for information disclosure from consumers. Blockchain is part of the solution to help manage transparency in supply chains in which brands can be ranked by how trustworthy they wish to be.

Sharing data in a decentralized ledger in which sensitive data, such as intellectual property, can be encrypted and securely stored allows all actors of the supply chain, such as farmers, manufacturers, brands and even customers, to opt in or out. However, it is the product itself that will carry the information as a form of digital DNA, containing proof of origin, quality, product compliance and authenticity to name just a few. The ongoing challenge is to find one single source of truth in the current competitive landscape which may create more silos, even in a distributed network.

Neliana Fuenmayor, founder of A Transparent Company, comments: 'As an industry with countless challenges, we need to accelerate positive impact in the value chain. Only with enabling technologies, such as blockchain, will we be able to add to proof of trust by increasing transparency and verified traceability'.

The fashion start-up

Whilst many of the larger fashion manufacturers and brands are now starting to understand the benefits of being more transparent in their supply chains and beginning to adapt their procedures, it has been start-ups that have been quickest to lead the change and disrupt the market. It is inevitable that larger companies will follow as consumers are increasingly voting with their wallets

One such company is BEEN London that produces sustainable premium fashion from products that have 'been' something else. All its raw materials are sourced from products that would otherwise have ended up in landfill. It's a point of difference at the core of its brand and ethos. When considering ways to prove it to customers, the founder quickly realized that the only way was to incorporate blockchain into the supply chain and let her buyers check for themselves.

BEEN London joined forces with A Transparent Company to implement traceability and increase transparency. From the outset, the whole supply chain has been on the blockchain, making it easy to scale as the company grows.

Any customer can scan a simple NFC tag on one of the company's bags. They can see the manufacturers of the leather and the lining, as well as anything else that has been recycled. The user can also see the studio where the bags are handmade and from where they are dispatched. All is visible, all is traceable and all is transparent with no doubts about the provenance.

Such a use of blockchain makes business sense, when consumers are prepared to pay more for products that are sourced ethically and protect the planet, if they can trust the claims that are being made. Genia Mineeva, founder of BEEN adds: 'if blockchain can help us all trace the full circle from waste to new beautiful products, then I'm excited about what we can do with it next'.

The new normal

Disruptive start-ups exist in any sector because they are more agile and quicker to see the benefits of doing something new or in a different way. By inventing new ideas or technologies, or by being innovative in the way that they adapt them for use in their own business models, they are able to scale quickly.

But it is not only their own growth that benefits from disrupting markets. By forcing more established players to look more closely at their own procedures and by offering consumers a choice of doing something in a different way, start-ups are able to help redefine entire industries.

Blockchain as a technology is itself redefining processes and procedures, as well as providing solutions where none existed previously. As in the case studies above, it is start-ups who are often its early adopters and responsible for speeding its spread.

Much has been said during the 2020 coronavirus lockdown about how the new normal might differ from what went before, but there is no doubt that blockchain is being adopted in ever wider ways in ever more industries, and this speed of change has been accelerated.

A Transparent Company is a London-based consultancy whose purpose is to accelerate positive impact in the fashion industry through sustainable innovation helping brands to become a transparent company, connecting physical products to digital stories.

BEEN London is a next generation global sustainable accessories brand, turning waste into premium products. It is the only brand making handbags entirely from materials that would otherwise end up in a landfill. Everything from zips to lining is made from recycled materials and all is tracked on blockchain, disrupting the global accessories industry by doing everything differently.

8.

BLOCKCHAIN: THE DIGITAL INFRASTRUCTURE

Mike Kiersey and Colin Bradley at Dell Technologies look at the options for a chief information officer in creating an end-to-end blockchain solution

Your organization has explored the business value associated with adopting a blockchain technology and it appears that there are significant business gains to be achieved. It is now over to you as CIO to put in place an end-to-end blockchain solution that will deliver these gains. Easy, right? Where do you begin? What principles do you use in your decision-making? And what infrastructure, if any, is required?

An obvious place to start and many do is to look at the variety of blockchain as a service (BaaS) offerings, such as Amazon Blockchain Templates, Baidu Blockchain Open Platform and Microsoft Azure Blockchain. With a cloud operating model these services can be easily consumed, but you need to consider the information/data that you will be putting out there in these public clouds. Perhaps regulation and compliance prohibit the use of public cloud providers or strategically your organization wishes to have absolute control over its blockchain network. So, let's draw a line in the sand now and say that you have been asked to implement the following:

- An on-premises, permissioned blockchain solution.

- It must be secure.

- It must be scalable.

- It must be able to integrate with legacy systems.

Let's review these elements in turn;

A permissioned blockchain solution

Deploying your own blockchain infrastructure typically means that the blockchain will be private, also known as permissioned. That is, write access is only allowed by a limited number of nodes (a node being a device on the blockchain network) and access to the network is only permissioned through some on-boarding process. You may decide to distribute your blockchain nodes across many data centres or across multiple virtual machines or in some cases containers. A minimum number of nodes will be required, and this is dictated by the blockchain distribution you use and the consensus algorithm employed by the distribution. The hardware components of the blockchain infrastructure are comprised of: network, server and storage. The server or compute layer will function for the most part as blockchain nodes. In some cases, these are called replicas, in that they hold a copy of the blockchain and some of these nodes can also have special functions. But today if we just acknowledge that these are compute nodes that each hold a copy of the blockchain, that is enough.

Ensuring that all the nodes in the permissioned blockchain network can communicate with every other node is essential. This is a distributed peer-to-peer system after all: communication and sharing of data over a network is critical to the operation of the blockchain. A permissioned blockchain may use a Byzantine Fault Tolerant consensus algorithm in order to achieve agreement on whether a block is good and correct and should be written to the blockchain. However, BFT algorithms are quite chatty and scaling of these systems becomes quite difficult. Having a dedicated secure and scalable software defined network begins to mitigate these issues. Selecting a scalable BFT, such as VMwares Project Concord, will allow you to scale without compromising performance or time to finality.

Depending on what you are moving on to the blockchain will determine whether or not you require some off-chain storage. Typically, blockchains don't consume too much storage: for example, bitcoin since its creation, reaching approximately 226.6 gigabytes in size by the end of June 2019, according to quartely figures from Statista.

Occasionally organizations will attempt to put some data on the blockchain that has no place being there. Take MRI scans as an example. These would consume gigabytes of space on the blockchain in what has been called blockchain bloat. A more elegant solution would be to store the images themselves off-chain on an object store that can store data ensuring immutability. A fingerprint of the stored image can then be stored on the blockchain.

A key factor in the blockchain infrastructure is building trust, through securing and protecting the components of the infrastructure.

A secure blockchain solution

A fundamental principle underpinning any blockchain solution is trust. How do you establish and maintain trust between nodes? Blockchain provides transparency to all parties in the consortium, even when in a trustless state. It is normally the role of the consensus algorithm to establish trust, ensuring that a block is valid and can be placed on the chain. But if we do not secure the infrastructure underpinning the blockchain from cyberattack then how can we trust the blockchain as an entity.

For example, one of the most well-documented and publicized cyberattacks is known as the 51 percent hack. This hack is particularly relevant to proof-of-work consensus systems, such as bitcoin, where the hacker needs to compromise at least 51 percent (hence its name) of the nodes in order to be successful. Developing a sophisticated multi-factor approach to security can greatly reduce the likelihood of a successful attack and minimize its extent and its impact if it were to occur. Ensuring the components of our blockchain infrastructure are protected from a cyberattack is critical to any blockchain strategy.

A resilient secure modern infrastructure is therefore needed. The security needs to be built from the ground up:

- Secure systems: security built into core servers and infrastructure.

- End point protection: protects and manages data on laptops, desktops, mobile and IoT devices.

- User access control: secures and manages user identities, access privileges and lifecycle.

- Network protection: makes your entire virtual network security aware.

Adopting a software-defined approach can better help you to implement a dynamic security posture that is adaptable to the ever-evolving threat landscape. In addition, it can reduce capital expenditure by minimizing the need for hardware devices such as routers and switches, as well as lowering operating costs due to simplification in managing the infrastructure.

A scalable blockchain solution

The problem of scalability has been a focus of intense debate, rigorous research and media attention for the last few years. It is the single most important problem that could mean the difference between wider adaptability of blockchains or limited private use by consortiums. From a theoretical perspective, the general approach revolves around protocol-level enhancements, for example:

- Bitcoin scalability is to increase its block size.

- Other proposals include off-chain solutions that offload certain processing to off-chain networks, for example, off-chain state networks.

- Infrastructure and the cloud.

Based on the above solutions, proposals can generally be divided into two categories:

- On-chain solutions that are based on the idea of changing fundamental protocols on which the blockchain operates.

- Off-chain solutions that make use of network and processing resources off-chain in order to enhance the blockchain.

However, recent papers suggest other elements that perform specific functions ought to be considered.

- **Networks**: the network is a key function to ensure transaction propagation. As identified in many papers and journals, network bandwidth is underutilized due to the way transaction validation is performed by a node before propagation and is duplicated, first in the broadcast phase and then after validating in a block.

- **Consensus**: this layer is responsible for validation and achieving consensus. Bottlenecks in this layer revolve around limitations in proof algorithms (proof of work, proof of state etc), whereby increasing consensus speed and bandwidth results in compromising the security of the network due to an increase in the number of forks.

- **Storage**: the storage plane is what stores the ledger. Issues in this layer revolve around the need for each node to keep a copy of the entire ledger, which leads to certain inefficiencies, such as increased bandwidth and storage requirements. In bitcoin, pruning is a method that allows a node to operate without the need to keep the full blockchain in its storage. This saves storage space. This functionality has resulted in major improvements from a storage point of view.

- **View and side planes**: which propose an optimization based on the proposal that blockchain miners do not need the full blockchain to operate, and a view can be constructed out of the complete ledger as a representation of the entire state of the system, which is sufficient for miners to function. Implementation of views will eliminate the need for mining nodes to store the full blockchain. Finally, the side plane represents the idea of off-chain transactions whereby the concept of payment or transaction channels is used to offload the processing of transactions between participants, but is still backed by the main bitcoin blockchain.

- **Infrastructure and cloud**: abstracting these can fundamentally help improve the performance of a blockchain deployment.

Finally, private blockchains are inherently fast because no real decentralization is required and participants on the network do not need to mine; instead, they can only validate transactions. This can be considered as a workaround to the scalability issue in public blockchains; however, this is not the solution to the scalability problem. Also, it should be noted that private blockchains are only suitable in specific areas and set-ups, such as enterprise environments where all participants are known.

As principal technologist and evangelist at Dell Boomi, **Mike Kiersey** helps companies become more connected in the digital era, primarily focusing on connecting disparate applications and data sets to blockchain and DLT technologies. Before joining Boomi, Mike was the global pre-sales director and CTO at Dell EMC, supporting 17 strategic global partners to develop end-to-end solutions to address the complex needs of being a digital business. Mike has broad industry knowledge with experience in government, defence, the law and finance. He has a master's degree in information technology and strategy, and a passion for emerging technology.

Colin Bradley has been in the technology sector for over 20 years, previously working at Lehman Brothers and spending over ten years as a vice-president in Citigroup's architecture and engineering department. Colin currently performs the role of field CTO with Dell Technologies in the UK & Ireland. He engages primarily within financial services, helping to expand the conversation with the C-suite and demonstrating how architectures based on Dell Technologies' solutions can help them achieve their business goals. Colin is particularly interested in emerging technologies, such as blockchain, quantum computing and AI. He has spoken at a number of internal and external events on the ethical use of AI in the modern world. Colin holds a diploma in applied physics and instrumentation and also a BSc (Hons) in natural sciences.

9.

BLOCKCHAIN AND THE CHANGING FACE OF PAYMENTS

The lockdown has accelerated the switch to digital payments, but who will be the first to resolve the challenges of operating blockchain, asks Robert Lincolne at PayDock

In its early years, blockchain may well have been regarded as a solution looking for a problem. Similar things were said of the laser the reader may recall. Relatively unproven and lacking adoption for the first five years of its life, today, blockchain is a different story. With over $23 billion of venture capital flowing into the sector (Outlier Ventures, 2019), blockchain is here to stay. Businesses who correctly understand the technology and its applications will be positioned to sustain a competitive advantage while reducing operational cost and risk. Amidst a sea of applications, one of the most promising appears to be payments.

The recent situation faced by the global merchant community as a consequence of coronavirus has no doubt accelerated the trend. Cash is less acceptable than ever, traditional point-of-sale has 'died', and the costs and risks associated with digital payments are less tolerable than ever. Blockchain has never been more relevant than in 2020.

Capitalizing on blockchain's value in payments is not without challenges. As with all innovation, incumbent vendors maintain substantial inertia and the weight of infrastructure will not be replaced quickly. Consumer habits will also take time to change, accelerated as they were in 2020. The presence of regulators, still seeking to understand broader risks, also factor into the future of blockchain, but to the winners go the spoils – and a race it is.

Two key drivers of profitability

Blockchain today encompasses a broad suite of use cases including rights management, personal data management, fractionalized asset ownership, supply-chain provenance and, of course, consumer wallets and payments. However, when it comes to blockchain, bitcoin, a payments proposition based on the technology, may be the most famous application.

Bitcoin has been cited as the most significant innovation in financial services since the arrival of the credit card and the appeal of fully traceable, near real-time, irreversible transactions is naturally significant. Today, 100 million bitcoin owners transact in excess of 230,000 times per day.

One might conclude the case for a revolution has been settled.

In a world where globalization has spread the links of trust and supply further and wider, the promise of blockchain to satisfy the requirements of both necessary trust and agreed exchange of value (at a fraction of the typical speed and cost) is intoxicating for any business.

A shift in trust

Solving the trust problem is at the heart of blockchain technology. Its inherent distributed trust capability resolves this, as any transaction can be instantly verified by any third party on the network. While great for consumers, this trust shift presents a challenge to some members of traditional payments value chains.

The role of incumbent identity and banking providers as a central trust hub has become threatened. If you have used Google Pay, Apple Pay or even PayPal, then you have relied on these providers to act as a traditional trust anchor within a transaction.

To complete a traditional transaction, you supply specific personal information to this third party to verify you are authorized to remit an amount of fiat (or non-fiat) currency, which is either validated by this party or not. You simultaneously hope this information will not be exposed or transmitted to third parties without your consent (though perhaps slightly less optimistically).

In a blockchain transaction a component of this

function is no longer required. The blockchain network itself provides programmatic (in fact, cryptographic) attestation to support the validity of the transaction. It is secure, immutable, transparent and traceable.

Imagine a hypothetical friend called Bobby. If in the real world, Bobby hands £10 to Kim, it becomes a fact of history, though possibly not externally verifiable. Kim may claim Bobby did not actually give it to her. In the blockchain world, this action can be recorded and verified globally and instantly.

Not the whole solution

Transaction validity is only half the equation however. While identity providers, as well as banks, face disintermediation, there is still required some form of mutually agreed trust anchor.

Referring to our £10 transaction. If Bobby was ten and seeking to purchase beer, the transaction may have been valid (it was £10 after all, which is an agreed exchange of value) but the action may not in fact be authorized.

Two questions must be resolved: first, how do I know the person giving me the £10 is authorized to give me the £10; and, second, how do I know the person I am sending the £10 to is authorized to receive it.

Ascertaining whether the identity of who is proposing the transaction is authorized to make such a proposition (valid or otherwise) has been one of the primary challenges in the payments application of blockchain. What members of the blockchain community have put forward include a new set of government, educational or societal trust anchors. Of special note is that these parties are political rather than commercial. It is hoped that identity data supplied or derived from these non-commercial parties is less likely to be exploited and treated as a commodity (remember Cambridge Analytica).

One further point applies to the two key principles of authorization and agreed value. Businesses today are developing innovative solutions either side of the problem without necessarily covering both (or having to). Therefore applications based on blockchain to remit payments without addressing traditional AML and KYC (anti-money laundering and know your customer) processes have been entering the market alongside separate applications to assist or re-think AML and KYC, while engaging traditional payment services. There are, of course, those that also seek to do both.

Where to next

We can confidently expect to see more and more blockchain-enabled payments as part of day-to-day life whether we know it or not. These providers seek to enable adoption without forcing merchants or even consumers to understand the intricacies. Their goal is to move the dial from 'confusing' to 'it just works'. Knowing that it's there, that it's safe and that it provides a substantial benefit to their bottom line is about as far as it will go for many.

The introduction of blockchain-enabled state-regulated identity services will be of particular interest in the next phase of blockchain. When we consider the two parts of the equation mentioned above we can see how it will be both valuable and potentially disruptive. Improvements to the tooling that supports the regulation of KYC, AML and counter-terrorism financing (CTF) also look promising, although the acronyms will remain.

Where should business look?

Blockchain has made enormous inroads in remittance, even while many coins are at an infancy stage. In the traditional payments industry, cross-border remittance is costly and expensive with many fingers in the pie. Intermediary banks, exploitative foreign exchange fees and legacy technology add cost and time to moving money.

Blockchain providers such as Ripple seek to escape this orbit. They have removed many of these layers and simplified the process of executing externally verifiable, intermediary-free, trusted transactions. They now offer secure, traceable and verifiable transactions to the payee, facilitator and recipient 'as service'.

As venture capital and alignment with non-bank trust anchors increases, we should witness exciting progress in addressing authorization and identity concerns. This will make increasingly tangible the promise of blockchain in our daily lives.

The response of incumbent consumer and banking

brands will be of interest to watch. Their value as a trust anchor and intermediary appears to be eroding and it remains to be seen what kind of legacy will endure. Some see little more than a relic of greed and exploitation while others hope that the inevitability of blockchain will empower the agile to benefit all, regardless of brand.

How are incumbents responding

Facebook's Libra experiment might give us an indication of how these older brands seek to leverage their footprint and maintain control of the consumer. Establishing themselves as a trust anchor and deploying intra-network currencies, they appear to demonstrate an awareness of the possibility of removing these incumbents (or repackaging them) and introducing scope to pressure regulators and other competitive threats when it comes to trade and commerce. The public headwinds faced by Facebook's Libra has been a testament to this, despite the official stance of neutrality and accountability.

Many feel that blockchain must return to its free and open roots. A blockchain project that holds sacred the concepts of self-sovereign identity via an open source base may be something that truly changes the world.

In its simplest form, access to personal information would be owned and managed by the holder of that identity. Third parties who facilitate transactions need only know the user is (a) authorized and (b) the transaction is valid.

Here we have a genuine need-to-know utopia, where only

what is absolutely necessary is available for the facilitation of the exchange of value or execution of a contract. And what is necessary is surprisingly simple and refreshing in a blockchain world when it becomes possible to abstract identity itself. To round out our £10 illustration, Bobby would simply be: 'an authorized person exchanging an agreed amount of value for an agreed result'.

Embracing solutions like this can help roll back the current proliferation and exposure of personal information and at the same time reduce costs for organizations seeking compliance with regimes such as the EU's GDPR.

The future of blockchain is compelling. The promise of equipping individuals and corporations to exchange value safely, faster and with lower cost than ever before is exciting. Consumers, corporations and government all stand to benefit. The implications for privacy are positive and, as a consumer myself, I am looking forward to a world with more ownership of my data and less value erosion across the payments stack. If ever there was a time to consider applications for competitive advantage now would seem it.

Who wins the trust battle and how the incumbents will work to maintain a grip on consumer data are fascinating questions yet to find their answers. I'm not placing my bets, but I hope in the end it's something that returns a little more control to us humans at the end of the pipe, whatever that pipe actually is. Watch this space.

Robert Lincolne is founder and chief executive at PayDock, an innovative payments orchestration platform focused on returning billions to merchants trapped in their existing payment systems. PayDock removes significant problems relating to fragmentation, cost and efficiency, and provides a compliant, interoperable framework as 'the last payments integration' a large organization or charity will ever need to make.

10.

BLOCKCHAIN AND ITS
LEGAL IMPLICATIONS

Charles Kerrigan of international law firm CMS reviews the legal implications of how blockchain is being deployed, how it will affect the practice of law and what it will mean for corporate finance

Doing their day jobs, lawyers will tend to come across blockchain technologies for one of two reasons. Their firm or a client may launch a blockchain project and they are asked to support it. Or a technical question may arise in a blockchain project that comes their way without much context or background.

Regardless of an individual lawyer's view of whether blockchain will change the world through the creation of new trust paradigms or is simply an oversold example of a database, it is necessary for lawyers to have at least educated themselves on the basics.

This chapter looks at the topic through three introductory

questions. What are the types of use cases that lawyers may see concerning blockchain? What legal issues arise generally on blockchain projects? What does blockchain mean for the job of a lawyer?

What are the types of use cases that lawyers may see concerning blockchain?

Most blockchain projects that a lawyer will see will fall into one of five broad categories:

- **Fundraising** will be one of two types: either an (unregulated) initial coin offering or a (regulated) security token offering involving the issue of tokens with characteristics that are similar to joining a club, owning either equity or a debt instrument or a hybrid.

- **Provenance projects** will be designed to satisfy a person (who may be a consumer or a business) at the end of a supply chain about the traceability of a particular asset. This may be because of incidents of fraud or counterfeiting in relation to a particular type of asset (such as diamonds or wine), or because a product is sold as having a particular history (such as coffee beans or olive oil), or because a supply chain has advertised certain environmental, social and governance (ESG) credentials.

- In **enterprise technology**, use cases relate to the

development of the technology itself. In the case of blockchain, it may be direct, such as a development in cryptography, or it may be indirect, such as the development of a method of storing digital assets that are generated by a blockchain.

- In **payments and settlement**, use cases arise from inefficiencies in traditional payments systems.

- **Policy** use cases focus on financial and social inclusion and aim to provide better government services.

Each of these raises completely different questions for a lawyer:

- **Fundraising** analysis is focused primarily on whether the transaction comprises an offer to the public of securities. If it does, it must either be described in a long-form public prospectus or it must benefit from an exemption, such as under the EU crowdfunding regulations. If it does not, few technical rules apply.

- In a **provenance** use case, a lawyer is focused primarily on the validity and integrity of information, regulated by contracts and sale-of-goods regulations in supply chains. While blockchain cannot help with poor historic data, it works well in situations where new data is created within the system, such as in industries that manufacture or process premium products.

- In an **enterprise technology** use case, a lawyer is focused primarily on the ownership, control and licensing of software systems, including both source and executable code.

- **Payments and settlement** use cases usually require a market solution for adoption across an industry. For this reason, they involve regulators and trade bodies. They also involve governance questions that are similar to those arising in joint ventures but with their own particular features. They are difficult to develop but then operate at scale. In the early stages, these types of projects often involve consortia.

- **Public policy** projects are special cases. They deal with real-world issues that can only be solved at national or international scale, such as digital identity. They involve hard technical, as well as policy, problems and involve work with standards and standards bodies. In these cases, lawyers are involved in social policy, procurement, legislative policy and some consulting work.

What legal issues generally arise on blockchain projects?

There are some difficult problems associated with blockchain projects as far as a lawyer is concerned. This is because the legal context is quite different to most traditional projects. For example:

- There is no direct regulation of blockchain technologies or applications in the United Kingdom and most other jurisdictions. Some jurisdictions do have a blockchain law which they advertise to promote themselves as friendly jurisdictions for projects. Generally, these laws are facilitative. They are designed to ensure that the mechanics of equity or debt or exchange laws allow for digital assets, rather than excluding them because the concept was not known at the time those laws were enacted.

- Blockchain projects are not confined to one jurisdiction where local rules can fully describe them. Most legal systems recognize assets by reference to the legal system of the location of the asset. Most blockchain projects are international in nature and it is sometimes difficult to determine the rules that apply to them.

- Projects involving financial assets or financial services are critically concerned with the regulatory perimeter that applies to them. This means that the project operates in a regulated environment and it is therefore critical to know which regulator and which rules need to be analysed in relation to it.

- Blockchain projects involve multiple parties, but are not developed in a way that is traditional for multi-party commercial transactions, such as a joint venture. Joint ventures are based on contracts between all of the parties. In a blockchain project, there may be no contract or it may be a smart contract code that runs the commercial arrangements.

- Most of the stakeholders involved in blockchain projects are not simply concerned about whether they are legal, but also about whether they conform to norms and standards. The role of standards bodies, such as the British Standards Institution in the UK and the International Organization for Standardization are important, but these bodies are likely to be unfamiliar to corporate and commercial lawyers.

These five examples (among others) indicate why lawyers need to adapt their usual approach when dealing with a blockchain project. In addition, specific technical points arise in blockchain projects. For example:

- In jurisdictions that now have a blockchain law, it is necessary for a project lawyer to have enough familiarity with the new law to ensure that the overall structure is compliant.

- When there is no specific blockchain law, jurisdictions are increasingly putting in place new rules relevant to specific use cases. For example in the UK, the Financial Conduct Authority has announced cryptoasset regulation that will impose obligations on providers of a broad range of cryptoasset services.

- The basic-sounding question of what is the legal nature of a particular blockchain technology can be difficult and significant. Depending on the particular characteristics of a technology and how the participants interact, the relationship may be rightly characterised as a joint venture, a partnership or a *sui generis* arrangement. Tax, accounting and legal consequences can flow from these distinctions, however, so they matter.

- Liability issues are significant in blockchain projects: partly as a function of the number of parties involved and the various ways in which they may suffer loss while the technology is operating; and partly as a function of the fact that the automated nature of the technologies can give rise to unintended consequences.

- Data protection and GDPR issues are part of every project. It is well known that the immutable and decentralized features of these technologies give rise to GDPR problems. These can be solved by design, consent or otherwise.

- Remedies are an open question for these projects. Contractual remedies are only appropriate if it is clear that the parties intend a contractual relationship to come into existence between themselves. Otherwise, tortious and equitable remedies may apply.

- Finally, blockchain projects provide the introduction for many lawyers to the world of smart contracts. The term, smart contract, refers to a piece of code that changes a relationship between parties, for example, the transfer of value once a condition is met. The English legal system (along with most others) is, however, still getting to grips with their legal status.

What does blockchain technology mean for the job of a lawyer?

It is clear from the points above that there are new projects for lawyers, new areas of law and new questions for existing areas of law. The question that is most often asked, however, is: will my job change or disappear?

It is clear that the job will change, but in ways that make it more interesting. In addition to handling matters arising from the technical points discussed above, projects involving blockchain technologies require the type of skills that lawyers are good at and trained for. Lawyers have experience in managing large projects with multiple stakeholders. That is almost always the case with a blockchain project. The projects also require close reading skills. Because the projects are designed to run on an automatic basis once started, it is critical that they are established with a high degree of accuracy and with a great deal of attention to the detail of each element and how these fit together. Lawyers are skilled in detailed review of complex statements, in considering and accounting for multiple possible outcomes and in being open minded about unintended consequences. Beyond the detail of individual projects, there are requirements for ensuring consistency between new projects and business-as-usual projects, for governance rules and policies, for adherence to standards as well as laws.

For some lawyers the most appealing aspect of working on these projects is collaborating with colleagues in different disciplines, including those involved in the deployment of frontier technologies in business. Blockchain is at its core an automation technology and automation projects naturally involve artificial intelligence, the internet of things, adoption of 5G and edge computing. There is a virtuous circle involved in use and development in all these areas.

We don't know how these activities will look in five or ten years. There are competing visions arrayed around a set of common assumptions and technologies. It gives rise to new types of projects, new ways of doing business and new technical and policy issues for lawyers. In my opinion, and looking just at the area I know best, it is likely that these technologies will change radically the operation of capital markets and markets for private debt. The same is likely to happen in all other transactional fields. The famous deflationary hammer of tech-enabled industry is coming to the industries that corporate finance lawyers inhabit. A small number of lawyers are already deeply involved in projects in this area and that number will only increase as the trend continues and evolves.

The Blockchain Industry Landscape Overview 2018 names **Charles Kerrigan** as one of the UK's leading influencers on blockchain. In 2019's Legal 500, he is described as 'the go-to person in the London market for funding intangible and digital assets'. He is a lawyer specialising in finance and technology at CMS. He works on fundraising transactions in corporate finance and venture capital for companies, funds, platforms and financial institutions, as well as on consulting projects on blockchain, digital assets, AI, automation and transformation for public bodies, policy-makers, standards institutions and corporate clients. He sits on the advisory boards of the UK All Party Parliamentary Groups for AI and for blockchain. For further details, see: www.cms-cmno.com.

11.

BLOCKCHAIN INVENTIONS
AND INTELLECTUAL PROPERTY

Richard Nugent at Coller IP and Totalinfo reviews the surge in IP filings for blockchain, particularly from China, and blockchain's impact on the process of innovation itself

Blockchain is a rapidly evolving technology with a diverse range of potential uses. This is clear. The concept of a distributed ledger being deployed in multiple industry sectors gives rise to a huge range of potential blockchain variants. In turn each of these variants and associated applications creates the potential both for IP rights, as well as an impact upon the world of IP.

IP relates to intangible assets and comes in a variety of forms, principally, copyright, designs, patents and trademarks. In a summarized form, copyright relates to the expression of ideas (eg, in a piece of writing, such as a book or expressed in other formats such as sound); design relates to the form of a product; patents relate to novel and inventive concepts capable of industrial application; and trademarks are signs or symbols, such as a brand image. Intangible assets (often discussed when IP is mentioned) also go beyond the core rights to include aspects including trade secrets and know-how amongst many others.

In addressing how blockchain and IP relate, this chapter will examine the following areas:

- Blockchain innovations to date (as demonstrated by known patent filings by February 2020).

- How blockchain innovation is impacting the world of IP.

Blockchain innovations

To assess blockchain innovations for the purpose of this article, we will look at those innovations that have been registered by companies and individuals on global patent registries. This provides a partial picture of blockchain innovation, as some innovations will either not be registered or not be visible on the public registries. There are many ways to search patent registries, whether through patent classifications, filtering across date ranges, searching key words or using semantic or even artificial intelligence powered techniques. Each method has its strengths and weaknesses, none are perfect.

For this article, to capture a picture of innovation a

keyword search strategy has been chosen, searching for the following: TAC_ALL: '(blockchain OR 'distributed ledger' OR 'block chain' OR 'block-chain' OR 'hash-based proof-of-work')'.

The above query captures the different ways in which blockchain is described and the search was made using the PatSnap search tool. The TAC reference denotes that the search covers only title, abstract and claims of the search, thus only those patents most focused on the search keywords will be shown. The search also only shows simple patent families and is designed not to double count patents in different countries derived from the same source. What we find is that there have to date been around 23,000 patent filings which come within the scope of the search query noted above.

It is a sizeable number of patents for a short period of time, especially when we consider that whilst the Satoshi Nakamoto paper may have been released in 2009, patent filings were minimal until they finally began to increase in 2015. After that, 2016 saw just under 200 filings and in 2017 filings rose to just under 4000 filings, then a huge jump occurred in 2018 to a little under 10,000. At the date of writing not all these 2018 filings are public yet, so this number is likely to increase. Early, and very incomplete figures for 2019, show 8000 filings published already and it is likely this number will surpass 2018.

The majority, 59 percent, of blockchain innovations to date hail from China: Alibaba leads the world in filings followed by Tencent. This is no surprise to anyone who has visited China and witnessed the huge interest in blockchain in the past few years within Chinese technology communities, which is notable given that ICOs (initial coin offerings) are not allowed in China.

Innovation focus

Globally, we see that innovations to date in blockchain are particularly focused around the following technical areas and international patent classifications:

- Payment architectures (G06Q20).

- Finance; insurance; tax strategies (G06Q40).

- Arrangements, apparatus, circuits or systems (H04L29).

- Arrangements for secret or secure communication (H04L9).

- Systems or methods specially adapted for specific business sectors (G06Q50).

To summarize, we see that innovation is growing fast and that it is focused on securing transactions and payments across a wide range of sectors with a focus on financial transactions. If we look at the history of blockchain and the ideal behind bitcoin (to obviate the need for central banks), the focus on finance is unsurprising.

As we look further into the future, if we can engage in smart contracts using blockchain, which can be connected to payment mechanisms, this creates a wealth of opportunities to add a new layer of security to global supply chains. This in turn enables commerce to occur more easily. The new layer of security that can be provided by blockchain allows transactions to occur more quickly (via smart contracts) and it allows valid participants in supply chains to associate themselves with a transaction in a way that is easier for other participants to verify.

An example would be in the food sector where blockchain is being used to apply a higher degree of security to purchases. Consumers can know where a food item has been sourced, and in the event of a problem, eg, an impurity in the food, the source of the problem could be quickly located, and the amount of waste (by being returned) would be limited only to food from problem sources, as opposed to the current practice of withdrawing huge amounts of stock from supply (just to be safe), despite most of it probably being fit for human consumption.

Blockchain impacting IP itself

Blockchain also has the potential to impact the world of IP, both the registration and trading of assets. Currently, whilst there are national patent registries for patents, trademarks, and design rights, many countries, with notable exceptions such as the United States and China, do not have national copyright registries for their nationals. As a result, private registries have arisen for creators to register their works with trusted third parties who can attest to the identity of a registrant of copyright content. Some private registries are based on blockchain. These include Copytrack which locates online content infringing your copyright, then enforces it on your behalf. Another company, Digital Proof, uses blockchain to provide objective confirmation of authorship, helping clients to protect their IP. As well as protecting copyright assets, Digital Proof enables inventors who have filed patents to use their platform as objective evidence of invention at a certain date, enabling companies to have more confidence in collaborating at an earlier time.

Elsewhere, since 2018, blockchain-based evidence has been accepted in legal cases, such as copyright infringement, at China's internet courts in Hangzhou, Beijing and Guangzhou. In this way we can see that blockchain has made a genuine impact on IP protection and enforcement. This impact is only likely to grow as blockchain matures and is embraced by more traditional institutions.

Aside from the registration and enforcement of IP, blockchain is now being used to facilitate trading of IP assets. IPWe, a platform based on the IBM blockchain is one such platform, enabling the purchase, sale and licensing of IP. Whilst IP online trading platforms are well known in the IP industry for their lack of meaningful success to date, it is possible that IPWe may buck this trend, as it is quite unlike traditional online IP marketplaces, given its use of both blockchain and AI to enable and support transactions.

Conclusion

Blockchain is a novel technology, which has been the source of tens of thousands of innovations, particularly since 2015. Blockchain innovations vary widely in quality and degrees of novelty. A person versed in the history of recent blockchain developments would likely find many of the inventions to be not at all novel and, of the many inventions filed since 2015, overlap is clearly an issue. These doubts aside, there are significant innovations occurring at great pace involving all the main sectors of the economy who are keen to blockchain their technical space. Just as blockchain affects other industries, it is impacting the world of IP with new solutions to old problems.

This is where blockchain works best, when it solves a genuine problem that an industry is facing. Randomly blockchaining an industry is not enough. Rather blockchain must also provide solutions to industry challenges and pain points, executing these solutions in a user-friendly fashion.

In the years ahead, blockchain innovations will continue to solve problems, whether with supply chain facilitation, generating private keys using quantum computing, or enabling parties to reach agreements faster through more secured means of contracting. As we all think about how to use blockchain, could we find ourselves providing new answers to untackled problems, thereby creating new blockchain IP? If we do, will we be like Bernard of Chartres, 'standing on the shoulders of giants', or will our invention or creation simply be another block on the chain?

Richard Nugent is head of strategy at Coller IP and managing director at Totalinfo. He is a highly experienced and well-respected IP consultant, adept at unlocking value for creative and innovative organizations.

12.

BLOCKCHAIN AND SUPPLY CHAIN MANAGEMENT

Robbie Moulding reports from the frontline of supply chain management on how blockchain is being adopted

This chapter addresses the promise of blockchain technology within supply chain management. It draws on in-depth interviews of 33 practitioners with direct business experience of blockchain, including senior and middle managers, consultants, blockchain developers and industry experts. The research was based on a detailed analysis of documentation and literature spanning over a hundred industry, government and academic sources.

This summary brings together a series of insights into how supply chain leaders and professionals can unpack blockchain's transformative characteristics and realize its value within their operations. Specifically, the following core points are explored:

- **What** is the current state of supply chain management today and what are the main pain points that exist?

- **Why** blockchain technology is being applied to and implemented in supply chain management?

- **How** can organizations explore blockchain technology in their own supply chains?

- **Who** is doing what to grow their businesses now and in the future?

What: the current state of supply chain management

Supply chains have become increasingly complex and internationally distributed over the past 50 years due to globalization, which has increased risks associated with co-ordinating and managing end-to-end processes. Depending on the type of product, the supply chain involves multiple stages, passes through various geographical locations, comprises various payments and invoices, and involves numerous actors. It has resulted in a convoluted chain of procedures, which has made it increasingly difficult to track, trace, and monitor the flow of goods from point of origin through to point of consumption. Therefore, as supply chains have moved towards more complex, global networks, the level of uncertainty has increased and the span of control has fallen, creating gaps and inconsistencies in governance, due to international borders with different rules.

As communicated by the World Economic Forum (2019)[1], a product which moves along the supply chain from point of origin to its final destination can pass through the hands of many organizations, with each holding their own version of the truth. The involvement of multiple stakeholders and increasing number of multi-party transactions has made operations complex, which is compounded by a large amount of siloed data. This fragmentation and lack of visibility creates pain points around:

- Traceability and provenance
- Transparency
- Trust
- Co-ordination
- Accountability
- Speed and agility

As we progress into the future, those organizations who have stronger, safer and more secure supply chains will outcompete those who succumb to, or are weakened by, such pain points. We can therefore envisage the survival of the fittest supply chains; those who can optimize the end-to-end value chain will reap the rewards, whilst those who do not adapt to technological changes and new processes or systems will be left behind.

Why: the promise of blockchain

A study by Deloitte in 2017[2] highlighted that blockchain has the potential to 'revolutionize the way different actors capture, communicate and access information on a secure, shared and transparent platform'. The intrinsic properties of blockchain, alongside the internet of things (IoT), can address existing pain points and challenges that organizations currently face. An ideal supply chain contains end-to-end visibility, flexibility, trust and governance. Today, sharing information and trusting either the information or other actors within a network can be a major challenge. This begs the question: what role can blockchain play?

First, let's understand IoT. Put simply, it is a network of internet connected objects, which are able to collect and exchange data. Examples are devices, sensors and actuators. These provide organizations with data points, which can create new insights that can develop and deliver better services and operations. The challenge for organizations is to figure out what to do with the vast amounts of data that IoT will produce.

IoT is transforming the supply chain. Traditionally, the flows in supply chains are linear. However, supply chains today have evolved into a huge, global ecosystem that has created non-linear, multi-tier relationships. Through IoT, different parties can connect across the network and work together in new non-linear ways by sharing data. Organizations can see and react to any variations which occur in the supply chain to increase efficiency and traceability, giving supply chain management a more dynamic and pro-active capability, as opposed to a static and reactive nature, in areas such as:

- Asset tracking
- Vendor relations
- Inventory management
- Connected fleets

Traditional ledgers between organizations are slow and manually intensive. They involve constant back-and-forth communications as each organization maintains its own ledger. It is a time-consuming and error-prone structure.

On the other hand, a distributed blockchain ledger enables all parties to use the same data set, providing one source of truth. This removes any data silos in the network and creates an aligned system, due to the shared visibility of real-time information and multilateral communication provided by one distributed ledger. It significantly saves time on communication and subsequent reconciliation between parties. The data is therefore more transparent, traceable and trusted, which enables organizations to orchestrate activities within the network with greater ease. It also removes much of the uncertainty which exists in transactions today, driving efficiency gains and transforming how organizations can work together.

Blockchain technology can be summarized into four key characteristics[3] which set it apart from most existing information systems designs:

- **Distributed and synchronized across networks:** blockchains share data between organizations, reduce reliance on third parties, enable peer-to-peer transactions and automatically update ledgers for all parties.

- **Execution:** blockchains are programmed to automatically initiate actions when certain conditions are met via smart contracts, settling transactions quickly and reconciling work seamlessly.

- **Consensus:** all parties agree that a transaction is valid before it is executed, which creates trust by preventing any inaccuracies or fraud, resulting in transparency and ease of audit.

- **Immutability:** any data entered is permanent, chronologically ordered and available to all on the network, leaving details of an asset through its life.

Therefore, the combination of IoT and blockchain is a perfect relationship. The outcome is transparent, traceable and more trustworthy data. It is shared among all participants in a secure and immutable manner. It enables the continuity of information between actors within a supply chain and is easily accessible. Therefore, it can help organizations mitigate risks inherent within their supply chains by providing a holistic, network-wide view of operations. The challenges of information sharing, end-to-end visibility and trust can start to be resolved. Consequently, blockchain has potential to reinvent business transactions, creating an environment of complete trust and transparency.

How: options for implementation

For any organization looking to implement blockchain within their supply chain, there are a series of steps to consider:

- **Take time to understand current weaknesses and risks within a supply chain.** Identify key pain points and assess how blockchain could help address each one. It's always the problem first and then the technology.

- **Design a clear, shared and understood strategy.** Each party needs to understand the strategy to enable blockchain to shine. Strategic coupling is key: technology must be aligned with the strategy.

- **Start small.** Select a pain point to resolve that is not too complex or costly, which will best leverage the characteristics of blockchain and demonstrate the added business value (set realistic expectations). Ensure all parties within the network understand the value of implementing blockchain and how they will work together.

- **Build and maintain an agile approach.** Don't be afraid to try and fail (observe, reflect and make). This methodology enables organizations to monitor and develop their blockchain strategy and quickly show tangible benefits.

- **Collaborate.** Blockchain is a team sport: engaging networks is a critical success factor. Architectural discussions around rules of governance and incentives play a vital role. Align interests and goals, adapting business processes within the whole network. Each party sees the opportunity, value and fit with its own strategy alongside the development of the ecosystem as a whole.

Through these actions run three golden rules: a business problem to solve; an identifiable business network; and a requirement for trust. If these criteria are not present, blockchain is not the right technology to use.

Who: those growing their business

As highlighted, blockchain is a team sport, requiring a network of participants to collaborate in new ways. Two examples follow of organizations that are exploring blockchain today.

IBM Food Trust

All parties can know the provenance, real-time location and status of their food products, for example, helping them to:

- forecast supply and demand more accurately;

- increase food safety and freshness;

- minimize waste;

- enhance brand reputation.

Blockchain facilitates these supply chain players to work smarter across a shared ecosystem, where process inefficiencies can be easily identified and bottlenecks can be eliminated, to optimize the supply chain for continuous growth.

Tradelens

Tradelens provides each entity involved in global trade the digital tools to share information and collaborate securely. The benefits of this are:

- connecting the ecosystem by bringing together all parties in the supply chain onto a single, secure data-sharing and collaboration platform;

- enabling the digitization and automation of cross-organizational business processes integral to global trade;

- fostering collaboration and trust by ensuring all transactions, documents and data are secure and auditable;

- providing seamless, secure sharing of real-time, actionable information across all parties.

For users of Tradelens, blockchain reduces friction and simplifies the process of trade, solving the problem of how to prove uniqueness and provenance of a digital asset.

Organizations that onboard a blockchain network are becoming more agile and responsive to their external environments, enabling greater operational efficiencies due to their ability to monitor and control transactions within their supply chain network, provided by more trusted and transparent data.

To conclude, if an organization is either not aware of how to build a blockchain solution or does not understand how to strategically apply blockchain, it risks playing catch-up in today's fast-moving and uncertain business environment. It is time to either disrupt the status quo or risk being disrupted.

Robbie Moulding, 23, is a supply chain project manager in a FMCG. His experience of blockchain stems from his MSc at the University of Leeds, where he completed his thesis, *The Promise of Blockchain and its Impact on Relationships between Actors in the Supply Chain: A theory-based research framework*. Alongside this, Robbie has contributed to papers exploring blockchain that have been submitted to various conferences as proposals for further research.

Notes

[1] *Inclusive Deployment of Blockchain for Supply Chains*, part 1: introduction, World Economic Forum, 2019: http://www3.weforum.org/docs/WEF_Introduction_to_Blockchain_for_Supply_Chains. pdf

[2] *Continuous interconnected supply chain: Using blockchain and internet of things in supply chain traceability,* Deloitte 2017: https://www2.deloitte.com/content/dam/Deloitte/lu/Documents/technology/lu- blockchain-internet-things-supply-chain-traceability.pdf

[3] *Four characteristics that set blockchain apart*, Pattison I, 2017: https://www.ibm.com/blogs/cloud- computing/2017/04/11/characteristics-blockchain/

13.

BLOCKCHAIN, SKILLS AND NEW MANUFACTURING MODELS

Blockchain is opening up new business models in manufacturing. The challenge is to adopt it at the right speed and scale, says Marcos Kauffman at the Institute for Advanced Manufacturing and Engineering at Coventry University

Universities are increasingly recognising that blockchain technology is the way the world will execute transactions globally in the future. According to a Gartner research report[1] the business value-add of blockchain will grow to $176 billion by 2025 and will then exceed $3.1 trillion by 2030.

As identified by the World Economic Forum (WEF) report *Blockchain beyond the Hype*[2], this technology is as much about change management, economics and business models as it is about technology development and adoption. As such, in order to adopt and benefit from blockchain, businesses and their workforces will have to adapt to the changing environment.

Furthermore, it must be recognized that with the emergence of blockchain, our nation needs graduates trained in the technology to meet the industrial demand for innovation to happen at an appropriate pace. In this context, we need expertise in a number of areas of development and applications, as well as different blockchain platforms.

Via teaching and research, universities can help businesses realize that blockchain can be used to reduce operating costs, develop new businesses models and provide services to new customers in new markets.

To unleash the power of blockchain, business leaders must first understand the concepts of how blockchain applies to their business, before engineering and software developers translate those concepts into systems and applications that can be deployed.

For technologies to make a substantial difference to productivity levels, an agile response is required from universities and other educational institutions, focused on preparing students with the skills and information to conceptualize business use cases and on producing technically inclined graduates to build and apply these systems.

Addressing the skills gap

One method to tackle the skills gap and support businesses in addressing these technological challenges is being adopted by a number of universities that have created translational initiatives to support the engagement and collaboration with industrial partners. The Institute for Advanced Manufacturing and Engineering (AME) is one of these initiatives.

It is a partnership between Coventry University and an industrial partner, located on its site. Known as the 'faculty on the factory floor', it allows students to engage directly with engineering and manufacturing to the benefit of themselves and the industry as a whole.

In this initiative, the university takes the technology roadmap of the industrial partner and tailors the curriculum of its engineering degree to develop skilled graduate engineers who can apply new technologies such as blockchain. In addition to teaching, the university also maintain a multidisciplinary team of technology specialists and professors who are working together in collaborative projects to develop new solutions for the industrial sector.

This initiative also promotes joint academic-industry technology events open to other industrial partners across the value chain. These events include blockchain technology talks with experts and simulation sessions to stimulate discussions and explore potential use cases.

Through these events the academic teams work with the industrial partners to select suitable technology use cases for collaboration projects funded via government research and innovation grant schemes such as Innovate UK projects.

In order to carry out this selection process both, academics and industrial partners utilize a multi-step approach that focuses on feasibility, technical assessment, business case and strategic intent. As a starting point, this approach is aligned to a comprehensive white paper recently published by WEF[3] providing a practical framework to help businesses identify the value of blockchain technology and build a corresponding business case. This should be the starting point for businesses and universities considering projects trialling blockchain solutions.

Feasibility

Each potential technology use case is assessed with the industrial partner in order to identify the effort required to pilot and implement the solution. This assessment normally includes training via CPD (continuous professional development) short courses aimed at familiarizing the industrial partners with the particular technology so that they can make an informed decision regarding the operational feasibility, the time frame and their skills gaps.

Technical assessment

The next step focuses on a technical validation that blockchain is indeed the best technology to achieve the objectives of the use case. This includes conducting technical due diligence, assessing the maturity of the technology and the team's skills and capabilities.

Business case

Once the feasibility and technical assessments are completed, the academic team works alongside the industrial partners to evaluate the business case to justify the investment in the feasible use cases. This step focuses on assessing economic viability from both a financial and risk perspective.

Strategic intent

Finally, each use case is subjected to an assessment of its strategic intent to ensure that the potential solution is aligned to the industrial partner's strategy. If a potential use case undermines or negatively impacts the existing strategy or policies, the industrial partner will have to decide on how to proceed before any effort is placed into the blockchain project.

Deployments of blockchain technology

As a result of this multifaceted engagement with industrial partners, the university has supported a number of projects trialling blockchain solutions that are already delivering benefits academically and industrially. Such deployments of blockchain technology can be replicated as industrial use cases.

Enhancing automotive component traceability

Automotive products are becoming more complex and manufacturers in this sector need to improve the ways in which product-related information is collected, processed and exchanged securely across complex supply chains. One of our industrial collaboration projects focused on the use of blockchain to provide an immutable, permanent digital record of materials, components and processes that allowed end-to-end visibility and providing a single source of truth to a tier one manufacturer and its value chain partners.

The use of blockchain in this project enabled the industrial partner to reduce the operational costs associated with integrating and maintaining multiple IT systems across the value chain, replacing them with an open source blockchain solution. Furthermore, the manufacturer also estimates a significant benefit in terms of risk mitigation related to product failure recalls. According to a study by Capgemini Research Institute[4], product recalls typically cost manufacturers $8 million, which could be mitigated (or avoided altogether) by better traceability systems.

Enhancing quality control in automotive manufacturing

In this particular use case, a team of computer scientists and manufacturing engineers worked together to trial a blockchain-based bill of quality. A bill of quality is typically a set of documents containing all the required quality checks for the production of a particular product.

Blockchain was used in this project to create an immutable and distributed set of documents containing all quality checks and production process data.

In this blockchain, each product order had a unique order number which was used to associate and automatically identify every inspection, process, transaction, modification and quality check occurring in the manufacturing process.

The benefits of this project included the simplification of quality-related data collection and analysis. It also reduced the need for audits by original-equipment manufacturer who received a report containing all the information related to the individual products.

Protecting manufacturers' intellectual property

Modern automotive manufacturers across the value chain recognize the need to protect and utilize IP as a source of competitive advantage. One of our collaboration projects included a pilot where blockchain technology was used to control the background IP introduced by businesses collaborating in a research project. It also allowed the collaborators to track the IP resulting from the project with an unprecedented level of clarity avoiding any IP disputes over ownership of resulting IP.

In the same project, our team of experts also considered a small pilot which enabled IP monetization through the use of blockchain technology. This pilot utilized the product model's definitions and bill of process (digital design and manufacturing files) held in the blockchain to be licensed directly to a manufacturer who executed the production process utilising the information from the blockchain.

New business models in manufacturing

Blockchain technology is the key to unlock a number of new business models in manufacturing. Models such as machine as a service (MaaS) where instead of selling production equipment, a machinery builder can charge a manufacturer for its use and for its output.

For example, instead of selling a 3D printer, the machinery provider can sell time on that machine or the volume produced. This approach reduces the upfront investment, improves levels of use and results in a better return on the asset.

However, to realize such benefits, manufacturers must advance use cases beyond the pilot phase and improve their understanding of the technology. A recent Capgemini report[5] shows that only 3 percent of organizations are implementing blockchain on a large scale. For end users, the roadmap to substantial adoption of blockchain technologies depends on a critical mass of skills and capabilities.

Future academic research will focus on the development and testing of more complex business models, such as MaaS, which can facilitate documentation management, performance tracking and IP management. Use cases will distribute and authenticate a single version of the truth across the value chain, automating use and payment for machines and services in smart contracts.

The full potential of blockchain depends on our ability as academics and industrialists to bridge the skills gap through collaboration, overcoming challenges such as the traceability of complex products, the integration of value chain systems, data sharing, adherence to quality and process standards, and IP protection.

In 2019, **Dr Marcos Kauffman** became the director of the Institute for Advanced Manufacturing and Engineering (AME), a unique partnership between Coventry University and partners from manufacturing industry, which was formed in 2013 with the objective of bringing together business, research and education to accelerate the development of graduates ready for industry and the commercialization of new technology in the manufacturing sectors. Marcos joined AME in 2016 as innovation and digital director. Previously, Marcos worked for ten years in the UK automotive manufacturing industry where he was responsible for solutions design and business improvement in production and research. Further details at: www. coventry.ac.uk/ame/.

Notes

[1] *Blockchain Business Value, Worldwide, 2017-2030*, Gartner forecast, 2017: https://www.gartner.com/en/documents/3627117

[2.] *Blockchain: Beyond the hype, a practical framework for business leaders*, World Economic Forum, 2018: http://www3.weforum.org/docs/48423_Whether_Blockchain_WP.pdf

[3.] *Building Value with Blockchain Technology: How to evaluate blockchain's benefits*, World Economic Forum, 2019: http://www3.weforum.org/docs/WEF_Building_Value_with_Blockchain.pdf

[4.] *Does blockchain hold the key to a new age of supply chain transparency and trust?*, Capgemini Research Institute , 2018: https://www.capgemini.com/wp-content/uploads/2018/10/Digital-Blockchain-in-Supply-Chain-Report.pdf

[5.] *ibid*

14.

CREATE AND TRADE
YOUR DIGITAL ASSETS

Free up your assets for growth by creating tokens on blockchain, says Mike Kessler at Kession

There are real reasons to tokenize securities. In this chapter, we consider the rationale for tokenizing an asset, which can include equities, bonds, commodities, funds, property, royalties and securitization vehicles.

Firstly, it is important to distinguish what a token or digital asset is. The token (which can be referred to as a token, unit or digital asset) is a derivative of the underlying security. It is created on a blockchain and effectively contains certain contractual rights that can be programmed into the token and is often referred to as a smart contract. This smart contract is the token and it represents the security which typically remains in custody or in another form of safekeeping.

When the security token is bought (and paid for) the token is transferred to the new owner, the transaction is recorded on the blockchain and the register is updated with the details of the new owner who is now the new beneficial owner of the underlying security.

This process of tokenization is applicable to all security types. We will start with the most commonly held security, equity, and then discuss other forms of security that can benefit from tokenization. Whilst we will not cover all asset classes the process of tokenization remains the same.

Equity

Listing an equity on an exchange is an extremely costly process and involves the use of several counterparties. Normally you would have to appoint lawyers, a corporate adviser, an underwriter, a bank and maybe a broker. All in all, the listing fee for an exchange itself is normally relatively low, but the fees for the intermediaries are normally prohibitive unless the listing is of a significant size, hence the reason most stock exchanges only want to deal with large companies.

Private companies find it difficult to trade shares and attract additional shareholders. Tokenization presents a solution to this problem. It is possible to place the shares of a private company (in the United Kingdom) into a nominee company. These in turn can then be tokenized and the ultimate beneficial owner can trade those tokens in a private market and find new investors more easily. The rights are more easily transferred through a token than a direct transfer of the shares themselves.

Another common problem in equity in general is that private companies find it difficult to transfer shares and sell to other counterparties. If a problem develops in a company, or between shareholders, then all too often it has an adverse effect on the company as the equity holders find it impossible to liquidate or raise capital to buy out other shareholders.

Once a company has tokenized equity, it is possible to cost effectively reward employees and pass shares to other people. If one person falls out with a business partner it might be possible to use the community to buy that person out of their shareholding, or it might give the owners an opportunity to cash in on some of their shares. This is facilitated through the use of a bulletin board, a bit like eBay, but for shares. A regulated entity might be required to facilitate the trade, but this could provide a more accessible secondary market than is currently available to most would-be investors.

Another factor is providing for an exit or partial exit. Most shareholders buy into an equity offering and find it incredibly difficult to sell to one or many people.

It is also worth considering two more security types that are not currently traded on any exchange: physical assets and royalties.

Fractional or shared ownership

Fractional ownership (fractionalization) for physical assets is not a new concept. Shared and syndicated ownership has been around for hundreds of years. Whether it was a collective agricultural scheme or a number of enthusiasts clubbing together to buy part ownership in a small plane.

By tokenizing assets, it is feasible to securitize them and convert an asset into a marketable security. In so doing a group of individuals can co-own a property, a piece of art, a historical artefact like a national heirloom or a racehorse. The list of assets is endless, but the concept remains the same.

In simple terms, a physical asset is divided into equal units. By breaking down the assets into a grid it is possible to sell those units to anyone. Owning a small segment of a painting gives someone the ability to say they own a Picasso or a property in Mayfair.

Many of these assets might not generate any income and therefore give no reasonable means of return for the asset holders. These assets are likely therefore to gain in value as the demand and scarcity increases, creating a potential gain, if the token or the asset itself is sold. Conversely as demand falls so will the price of the token.

The ability to tokenize an asset gives the owner a way to raise capital for something they never thought imaginable. It takes away some of the professional middlemen, which affects the price paid for the actual asset in the first place. Professional fees should be reduced by creating standardized contracts. By providing a simple ownership structure, recording the ownership on the blockchain and having a token to represent ownership, people gain the ability to do something they never did before in these assets – trade.

A person, a company or a foundation can buy a tiny percentage or a large portion of an asset for whatever reason appeals to them. No longer does someone have to be wealthy to buy a stake in a property or a piece of art. Geographical boundaries should also disappear. These tokens should all be easily exchanged on a secondary market to allow a new shared asset economy to flourish and to empower people to raise money or sell assets in a way that was never previously accessible. The emergence of this new shared asset ownership is now upon us.

Royalties

According to Investopedia: 'a royalty is a payment to an owner for the ongoing use of their asset or property, such as patents, copyrighted works, franchises or natural resources. The legal owner of the property, patent, copyrighted work, or franchise receives a royalty payment from licensees or franchisees who wish to make use of it to generate revenue. In most cases, royalties are designed to compensate the owner for the asset's use, and they are legally binding'.

The concept of a royalty payment is nothing new. People have seen it in music and films for decades. What most people don't consider is that a royalty is a security. Third parties pay authors, musical artists and production professionals for the use of their copyrighted material. In the oil and gas industries, companies provide royalties to landowners for permission to extract natural resources from their property.

Effectively, the right to receive revenue is commercialized and structured into a contract. The price of the token might fluctuate, as might the demand to own a percentage of a company's profits. I use the analogy that I would rather have one percent of the profits of Apple than one percent of their equity. That way I am not subject to the directors deciding whether or not to pay a dividend. As a royalty token holder, I would have a contractual right to receive my one percent.

The advantage to the issuer is they do not have to give away equity in their business and it is a purely commercial transaction to receive monies in advance that can pay for upgrades to their sites or equipment. Unlike a variable coupon bond, there is no redemption period and it works in perpetuity. It can be advantageous for both parties, insofar as there are no conditions that put an obligation to repay or an expiration date. Effectively, it is a continuing obligation for the life of the issuing entity. At the same time, if the company wants to stop the arrangement, it will be obliged to repurchase those tokens on the market and therefore buy back its own income rights.

Conclusion

Tokenizing an asset and listing it on a regulated security token stock exchange can significantly reduce the overall cost of listing by removing intermediaries and automating processes. Indeed, it is far more efficient to trade and settle tokens than traditional forms of securities and, further still, the blockchain provides an immutable record of the transaction, ensuring the finality and auditability of the trade.

Whilst we cannot profess to give tax advice, tokenization may create certain future tax advantages, whereby the security remains in place, but the ultimate beneficial owner changes, therefore it may not be subject to a transfer tax.

Similarly, tokenization helps make listings on regulated exchange easier. Blockchain provides the ability to track the security and ownership rights as well as to trade 24/7, as well as reducing costs and finding additional investors who support this new asset class.

So ultimately what does tokenization of a security assist? While it does not in itself make a market, it makes the market more accessible through the reduction of cost, the automation of processes and the provision of frictionless trading underpinned by a secure and immutable record of transactions. While a token cannot create a buyer or seller, it increases the possibility of finding a counterparty by making the tokens accessible through a regulated stock exchange or marketplace.

Mike Kessler at Kession is an authority on tokenized securities and using blockchain on stock exchanges. He regular speaks at industry events with regulators, governments and exchanges on creating bridges between digital assets and regulated markets. Since 2018, he has been working with the regulator in Barbados and, in July

2019, the Tokenise Stock Exchange received a licence to become the world's first fully regulated dedicated tokenized stock exchange. It is a regulated multi-jurisdictional platform with a unified global single order book. Tokenise received its brokerage licence in January 2020. Additional licenses are being sought in several other jurisdictions. After qualifying from the University of Manchester in 1995, Mike built his career in investment banking, hedge funds, compliance and private equity.

15.

SMART CONTRACTS AND THE TRANSFER OF BUSINESS LOGIC

Troy Norcross at Blockchain Rookies reviews how smart contracts are evolving to transfer business logic into blockchains with speed, security and transparency

Smart contracts are an essential concept in the field of blockchain and distributed ledger technology (DLT). Where blockchain records ownership and transfer of assets between parties, smart contracts automate the transfer of assets in a way that is safe, secure, automated and without the need for third parties.

A simple way to think about smart contracts is to compare them to macros in a spreadsheet. A macro is a computer program which, when executed, updates the contents of the spreadsheet. Similarly, a smart contract is a computer program which, when executed, updates the contents of the blockchain.

Just as with blockchain transactions, smart contracts are immutable (unchangeable) and anyone with read permission can view the underlying code. Each member of the network who has a full copy of the blockchain also has a full copy of the smart contracts. No one version of a smart contract can become corrupt or modified by a single party.

When writing a new entry to the blockchain, the network must reach consensus to verify and validate the transaction before it is committed to the ledger. Similarly with smart contracts, the network must come to a consensus on the results of a smart contract before updating the ledger. To put it another way, multiple computers on the network all run the macro, and they all achieve the same result to reach consensus and update the ledger accordingly.

When executing a smart contract on a public permissionless blockchain, like ethereum, we are asking the network to provide access to computing resources, and we must provide an incentive for the network to process the smart contract. Each time we call a smart contract, we need to make a micropayment to cover the costs of executing our contract. In ethereum, we refer to this as the 'gas fee'. By applying a gas fee, the network ensures that no one abuses the network, and it also acts as a safety mechanism for runaway programs which might use excessive resources.

Smart contracts allow for the implementation of business logic into a blockchain to achieve the benefits of speed, security and transparency of transactions and to do so without the need for third parties.

Origins and protocols

The concept of smart contracts was initially discussed in a white paper in 1997 by Nick Szabo. Providing self-executing and self-enforcing digital contracts and attaching them to real-world assets eliminates many of the challenges of traditional contract execution today, including conflict resolution, contract breach and subsequent enforcement.

In 2013–14, Vitalk Buterin co-founded the Ethereum Foundation and launched the ethereum distributed computing network. Ethereum was the first blockchain to allow for smart contracts within an ethereum blockchain environment. Subsequently, numerous other blockchain and DLT protocols have created their implementation of smart contracts, including EOS, NEO, Tron and, most recently, Libra. As with any emerging technology, there are fierce opinions as to the supremacy and limitations of each.

Today's smart contracts use various languages specific to the individual protocol. Ethereum-based smart contracts are written in Solidity or Go. Libra proposes to use Move as its language.

The majority of early smart contracts operated as an automated form of escrow or trust. When an instance of a smart contract executes, the contract is funded with sufficient ether or other cryptocurrencies so that when the necessary conditions are satisfied, the funds transfer to the correct parties, including the possibility of funds returning to the originating party. Without being funded, smart contracts can't complete with assurance.

Connecting to the outside world

Self-contained smart contracts can operate straightforwardly. They have all of the information necessary to evaluate themselves and update the ledger. For example, did Susan send the correct amount of ether to buy her cryptokitty? If so, then transfer the cryptokitty to her wallet (CryptoKitties, https://www.cryptokitties.co/). But what if one or more conditions of the contract rely on information not on the ledger?

For example, an insurance company creates a smart contract which will pay out to the consumer if their flight arrives more than 30 minutes late. David buys the insurance by sending ether to the smart contract and then goes on his holiday. Unfortunately, David's flight is late, and he doesn't arrive until two hours after the initially scheduled time. How can the smart contract check the arrival time of the flight against the scheduled arrival time to determine if the policy should execute and David be paid the agreed benefit?

Enter oracle services. An oracle service is one that runs outside the blockchain environment and can both provide answers to questions as well as receive information from a smart contract to affect something in the real world. Oracles can either be software such as a website, hardware including IoT sensors or devices, or even real-world human beings.

From our example above, the smart contract knows the intended arrival time for David's flight. At 30 minutes past the intended arrival time, the smart contract calls an oracle service to determine if the flight arrived on time. If not, the smart contract executes and transfers a fixed amount of ether to David's wallet. The same smart contract might also send David a link to a pre-paid hotel room included as part of the insurance policy.

Each of the parties in the contract must agree to the use of the oracle service and agree to be bound by the information it provides. In some cases, the oracle service has a system of decentralized data collection and reaches consensus on an answer to a specific question. For example, what was the average temperature across London yesterday? The oracle service might check hundreds of sensors with multiple readings throughout the day before coming to an answer.

Smart contracts and bugs

As we have discussed, smart contracts are computer programs. And sometimes computer programs contain coding errors which result in undesirable results. Bugs are an unfortunate reality in the world of software development. When it comes to bugs in smart contracts, there are some additional layers of complexity and risk.

Due to the nature of smart contracts being open and transparent to the participants on a specific blockchain, it means that everyone can see the code. In public and permissionless blockchains like ethereum, this includes black-hat hackers who are always on the lookout for opportunities to exploit a bug in a smart contract under the hopes of stealing cryptocurrency. One of the highest visibility bugs occurred in a smart contract used by the DAO (Decentralized Autonomous Organization, an ether investment fund). In this case, the hackers stole 3.6 million (worth nearly $70 million at the time).

Please note that while there have been cases of bugs in smart contracts, the underlying ethereum protocol has not been hacked. The integrity of the ethereum blockchain has not been compromised since its inception. Similarly, the bitcoin blockchain and protocol maintains its integrity. The underlying consensus algorithms and cryptographic structures linking blocks in the blockchain ensure the security of the data and the network.

Legal implications of smart contracts

As smart contracts become mainstream, there are questions about their legal enforceability. The United Kingdom is positioning itself as a leader in smart contract law and the creation of legislation governing their execution. Three key areas are currently in focus: acceptance of immutability; futureproofing against changes in the law; and liability in the event of failure, error or breach.

Acceptance of immutability

The premise of immutability is that once information exists on the blockchain that information is immutable. It cannot be modified or deleted. Information written onto the blockchain is in chronological order so all entries are time ordered. This combination of chronological ordering and immutability is key to cryptocurrency transactions to prevent the double-spend problem.

A question that has not yet fully been worked out through the courts is whether or not data stored in a blockchain is admissible as proof in a case. If you are writing a new screenplay, you can register that screenplay with your name and identity and create an entry in the blockchain to show that it was your work as on a specific date. It is not unlike the old-style approach of posting yourself a copy of the screenplay and keeping the sealed envelope with the postmark. The question for blockchain and smart contracts is this: will the courts accept an entry in an immutable blockchain as a proof of prior art?

Futureproofing against changes in the law

A smart contract written in 2019 is perfectly legal, valid and binding. In future, the law could change to make one or more conditions no longer legal, or it could be that one or more parties to the contract are no longer allowed to engage in that transaction. The smart contract is immutably written into the blockchain, meaning it cannot be changed, thus creating a challenge. Building in special conditions to allow for revoking or expiring smart contracts is currently being explored.

Liability in the event of failure or breach

Liability is a crucial aspect to modern-day contracts. In regards to smart contracts, there are further questions of liability. If there is a bug in the smart contract, who is liable? The developer? The tester? If there is a breach of security or protocol in a public permissionless blockchain, for which there is no single entity in charge, who is liable? One thing is sure, lawyers around the world are looking into these situations and many others. Getting reliable answers will help smart contracts adoption to grow.

In summary

Smart contracts are neither particularly smart nor are they, on their own, contracts. Smart contracts are computer programs that reflect a contractual agreement between parties which executes on a blockchain in a safe, secure, transparent and efficient fashion without the need for a third party. As blockchain, smart contracts and the business/legal environment around them evolve, we will see continued growth in placing business logic onto the blockchain.

Troy Norcross is co-founder of Blockchain Rookies and former chief executive of Opengoods. Focusing on the business opportunities created by blockchain, Troy separates the value from the technical delivery of blockchain projects. With a background ranging from software development for flight simulators to running his own start-up focused on permission marketing, Troy has a wealth of experience across multiple industries. Hailing originally from 4000 acres of farmland in Missouri, Troy has lived in Amsterdam, Munich, Helsinki and currently resides in London. Troy's breadth of experience provides a unique perspective when looking at how blockchain can be applied to a business opportunity or to an industry at large.

16.

CUSTOMER LOYALTY
AND SMART WALLETS

At interfaces with the customer, blockchain is creating
new data points and rewards. Kate Baucherel reviews
the lessons from early adopters at Jaguar and in gaming

One of the greatest challenges of digital transformation is the need to identify and reap the benefits of new and unexpected behaviours. The secondary effects of solving a current business problem may be significant and unlooked for. Among notable early efforts to computerise business processes, Visicalc's first spreadsheet programme, launched in 1979, was developed to improve the burdensome and error-prone task of erasing and recalculating cell values with every change on a manual sheet. The unexpected consequence was a paradigm shift in the role of accountants: the combination of time on their hands and a powerful calculating tool transformed the finance function from bean counters to analysts.

When the internet first penetrated our homes and offices, few of us could conceive of the upheaval in communication and content sharing which followed, and the new world of social media which we now take for granted. The speed of change we now experience in the business environment, combined with the advent of powerful and disruptive technologies, including blockchain, means that successful enterprises must reach into an unknown future to grasp new opportunities for their very survival.

Maintaining customer loyalty

Schemes for customer retention are all around us. Our wallets and keyrings once bristled with supermarket, clothing store and coffee shop cards, and most have now been replaced with handy apps. Regardless of medium, such loyalty schemes are effective and useful tools for the retailer. The most sophisticated allow data to be gathered about buyer behaviour, and the simplest are designed to lock the user into continued custom, for instance by offering a free coffee with ten purchase proofs stamped on a card.

Existing technology allows these features to be improved in a linear fashion. Data collection becomes easier and broader with apps and location services that increase the data points around a purchase. Loyalty rewards are enhanced beyond 'buy ten, get one free' to targeted upsell across the retailer's range and even third party 'partner rewards'. It's an established system, but there are pain points for all participants in the existing process. Reward schemes are ripe for disruption and transformation, and current initiatives in blockchain can transform the customer loyalty landscape:

- Blockchain is being used in multiple settings to expose new data points, delivering greater value to the retailer.

- Rewards can accrue for activities beyond simple purchasing, building new loyalty incentives and increase customer retention.

- Innovations in gaming are primed to improve the experience of third party suppliers of rewards and consumers themselves.

It's all about the data

In April 2019, Jaguar Landrover launched the first proof of concept of its blockchain-based loyalty scheme. The headlines were firmly aimed at the consumer, revealing that car owners could 'earn cryptocurrency and make payments on the move'. Use of the JLR smart wallet in its fully realized future form to pay for tolls, parking and electric charging through a network of sensors promises to deliver a seamless customer experience with loyalty rewards building up in the background.

This is nice to have for the consumer, but also delivers a substantial commercial advantage to the business by exposing a complex matrix of new data. The data piece goes a lot further than purchasing behaviour: JLR's vision is of their vehicles playing an integral role as data gatherers in the smart city of the future.

The idea that private cars could be equipped to report live road conditions is just a small step from existing crowdsourced satellite navigation systems like Waze or the scanning vehicles that already roam our streets checking for potholes, but the ability to link data collection to a vehicle owner and reward them for their efforts is a giant leap. It opens the way to blockchain-enabled earnings for the consumer and a huge data resource for the enterprise.

Under the hood

Behind the scenes JLR has implemented the IOTA Tangle: this distributed ledger has a unique structure specifically designed for machine-to-machine transactions, enabling the sensors of the internet of things to collect and send data to its destination without human intervention.

Transactions are written to the ledger and attached to others by an edge, rather than forming a linear chain. A transaction can only be entered if the node doing so validates two adjoining transactions. This results in a random consensus where, as more transactions are entered, more validations are completed, so the system is expected to run faster the more data is recorded. The validations use the same hashcash algorithmic basis as the bitcoin blockchain but with a much lower level of complexity, which means that nodes can validate with lower processing power in the connected devices themselves or on smartphones or a vehicle's onboard computer. There is no mining involved and no transaction fees are charged.

IOTA's work with JLR is just one of the projects in their extensive portfolio. Their work demonstrates both the importance of blockchain to the management of the IoT and the importance of the IoT to our confidence in the data recorded on immutable ledgers. The volume of reliable data that can be harvested from an IoT-enabled reward mechanism opens doors for enterprises, giving them the tools to respond with agility to a rapidly changing market.

Transforming partnerships

As loyalty mechanisms become more sophisticated, so the consumer will demand a better experience. Partner programmes are an increasingly common model for customer retention, offering a wider range of rewards to the consumer while partners gain access to a large market through association.

There is, however, a recurring pain point in the process that becomes obvious as soon as customers engage with the programme and partner organisations to redeem their rewards. Points earned through qualifying activities must be converted to a voucher, once paper, often now electronic. The voucher must be presented to the partner in lieu of normal payment methods. The partner then has to process the voucher through its own business systems. It is an administrative headache that all parties tolerate in the absence of a better alternative.

Interoperable tokens

Blockchain offers a new approach. The use of interoperable tokens has emerged in gaming and is tailor made for this business challenge. Tokens are, quite simply, programmable money, and can therefore be designed as a piece of software which sweeps up these troublesome manual steps and interfaces.

Replicating existing mechanisms within a retailer's own systems is straightforward. Reward points earned can be represented by a token with specific properties: let's call them 'clubcoins'. In the retailer's check-out system, a clubcoin is generated against purchases and added to the customer's wallet. Clubcoins in the customer's wallet can be presented in payment, with the check-out system recognising the token and applying any special terms such as double points rewards or offers on goods.

This is familiar ground, but what if the customer wants to redeem a partner reward? Instead of obtaining and processing individual vouchers, the clubcoin's programming can be interpreted directly by the partner's own check-out system. Existing data collection is unaffected; indeed, additional data points can be exposed throughout the redemption process. Data is more reliable as software can be trusted to follow specific conditions, for example, where a token redeemable against a set menu should not be accepted for drinks or *à la carte* items.

Cash, coins and cats

As an abstract concept, interoperability can be hard to grasp, so let's look at how gaming has developed this function. This tale of digital cats requires a refresher on the nature of tokens.

Many commercial blockchain applications are using what is known as an ERC20 token, colloquially an 'alt coin'. (ERC stands for ethereum request for comment and refers to the relevant discussion in the open source community that led to the development of each type of token.) ERC20 tokens are programmable cash and they are 'fungible', or interchangeable with each other like a pile of bank notes from which you can draw any note at random to make a purchase. Our generic clubcoins would be fungible, each one worth the same as any other.

Games led to the development of the ERC721, a one-of-a-kind token, where each has specific and unique characteristics. These are commonly known as non-fungible tokens or NFTs.

The first high-profile blockchain game, Cryptokitties, uses ERC721 NFTs. This collecting game allows players to buy, sell and breed cartoon cats. Every cat exists as a token that contains its unique genetic traits: the code which gives an individual cartoon purple paws and curly whiskers, for example. The value of each cat varies according to the traits encoded in the token.

Both ERC20 and ERC721 could be useful to us, so we need a way to manage them: ERC1155 is a useful hybrid which combines both fungible and non-fungible token types under a single banner. In a rewards programme, this would enable us to give customers both standard clubcoins and special reward coins with unique properties.

How do these tokens cross into other systems? Cryptokitties has partnered with games built by different companies, allowing their NFTs to be represented in a new context. In the card-collectible game, Gods Unchained, each Cryptokitty token generated a unique card pack. In Battle Racers, the token generates a race car with the cartoon traits of the specific Cryptokitty.

In our rewards program, a token becomes a set-menu coin when it is presented to the partner restaurant and pays the correct portion of the bill in the restaurant's systems. The process is automatic and seamless, satisfying the needs of both customer and partner, building their loyalty.

Moving forward with blockchain

Blockchain is the tool that enables businesses to harness the IoT to gather data and to use interoperable tokens to improve the experience of customers and partners. Effective implementation relies upon clear understanding of existing pain points and potential benefits.

The first step for transformation must be a clear analysis of the loyalty scheme's process flows to highlight where real benefits can be reaped. Organizations should also define the current data points throughout their scheme and explore what additional data will be exposed through implementation of a distributed ledger. The work of big cats and cartoon cats has laid a clear path to future rewards for everyone involved.

Kate Baucherel is a business development and strategy consultant specializing in the application of emerging tech in business, particularly blockchain and distributed ledger technology. She has held senior technical and financial roles in businesses across multiple sectors, leading several enterprises through their start-up and growth phases. Kate's writing encompasses the factual and the fictional. Her books include *Blockchain Hurricane: Origins, applications and future of blockhain and cryptocurrency* (Business Expert Press, 2020) and the SimCavalier series of futurist cybercrime thrillers (Sixth Element Publishing).

17.

PLUGGING INTO THE BLOCKCHAIN ECONOMY

Robert Learney, head of distributed systems at Digital Catapult, discuss how the blockchain economy is taking shape and how to access its ecosystem

The world of blockchain has already attracted many talented individuals from across a broad spectrum of backgrounds. This range of individual stories has led to a flourishing of new businesses and offerings, filling a variety of niches to round out a rich ecosystem.

Many people face difficulties when first forging a path into these new territories. This chapter presents an overview of the structure and role of major sectors and parties active in this seemingly opaque area. The notes on relative global importance within the ecosystem are likely to be out of date in a few years, as international agreements and domestic policies play a strong role in encouraging or discouraging certain blockchain-related businesses from forming and growing in different jurisdictions. It should also be noted that this chapter has been written from a largely UK perspective, although many elements translate outside these borders.

Emerging subsectors

A 2018 national survey of the UK blockchain ecosystem undertaken by the London-based Digital Catapult identified four major subsectors and roles within the blockchain economy. There is some overlap between these, but by and large these descriptive roles apply across the globe.

The blockchain builders

These are the groups investing time and effort to build the structural elements of new distributed ledgers upon which others can then innovate to deliver user-facing interactive systems.

Some names may be well known even outside the sector: bitcoin, ethereum, Hyperledger (actually a collection of fundamental technologies rather than a single product), perhaps even R3 (the developers of Corda) and EOS. But alongside these major names are tens if not hundreds of other groups developing equally distinct distributed ledgers: Tendermint, Monero, PivX, Dfinity, ActiveLedger and many more.

Why, you may ask. If bitcoin defined the blockchain and ethereum showed how it can be programmable, why do we need so many different teams working on so many different protocols? The short answer is that it is an evolving field and nobody knows the right answer to the issue of distributed consensus.

The long answer is that these teams are often developing elements of technology for functionality not provided by other shared ledgers, whether that is privacy (eg, Monero seeks to build a bitcoin-type public permissionless ledger with absolute privacy), scalability (EOS and DFinity are pursuing transaction-rate scaling and computation, using new consensus models and cryptographic primitives respectively), or compatibility with enterprise working practices (eg, Corda from R3 or Hyperledger Fabric from IBM). Each team has something to add to the global conversation at this time, but getting under the skin of a particular offering often requires specialist knowledge and prolonged research.

The dApp cometh

If blockchain builders are busy creating the foundations of this ecosystem, those writing distributed applications (dApps) are engaged in making the technology useful.

The idea of a separation between centralization and decentralization at the application layer is another new concept the blockchain world has given back to the rest of the software industry. But what makes an application distributed? In the traditional software model, whether running on your laptop or in the cloud, a user usually has no guarantee over the visibility, irrevocability, method-of-state calculation or the data from which this was derived. In the dApp model however, the data, the code, and the computations are provable to all. It must be noted that correctness is a separate issue.

This is in keeping with the fundamental mission of blockchain technology to transform trust relationships. A trader telling you how they calculated the price of a derivative may be deserving of your trust, but walking you through their exact data and computations is a radically new way of guaranteeing it.

This part of the ecosystem is the one that grew fastest during the 2017 ICO boom.

Centralized providers

This tends to be the group most usually associated with the blockchain ecosystem: the companies who manage cryptocurrency exchanges or wallets. It must be noted that some of these services can however be decentralized. The important distinction is in who manages the access to the underlying decentralized system (the blockchain or ledger). If it is disintermediated and the individual can directly access the ledger or use a transparent dApp, it is decentralized. If however the route to finality and state update on the ledger is managed by an intermediary then it is a centralized service. This is no different from the paradigm of traditional banking. If you hold your cash, it is decentralized because you can access the financial system under your own terms. However, making international payments or trading shares through a provider requires you to give over control and trust in a third party.

Service providers

The fourth and final major sector within the blockchain economy is service provision. This includes a range of activities complementary to those in the other three sectors, such as blockchain-sector-specific marketing, research, investment, development consultancy, education, banking and others.

In terms of the number of individual companies active in each of these sectors, service provision and dApp development appear to be larger than centralized services, which in turn is larger than blockchain building. This funnel is as expected, as blockchain development is a specialized activity requiring highly technical skills, and managing centralized exchanges is highly regulated. The other two sectors require less intense oversight and can draw on more generalized skillsets.

Global activity

Now that we have an overview of the composition of the overall ecosystem, we can highlight some of the major activities occurring worldwide. These are somewhat broad brush, but reflect the major activities in each of these places.

United Kingdom, Singapore, United States

These countries have strong financial service backgrounds, which is reflected in the activities within each of their blockchain sectors. London is home to the majority of the UK's blockchain companies, of which the majority are developing financial service applications. It also serves as the global headquarters of some major blockchain groups including R3 and the Enterprise Ethereum Alliance.

Singapore's blockchain sector is also largely pursuing financial service applications, including the frameworks required for issuing centrally banked digital Singapore dollars on a blockchain.

The range of blockchain activity across the US is as diverse as the nation itself: some jurisdictions ban elements of it outright and others appear highly permissive. New York is matching London for its interest in financial service applications, and San Francisco and nearby Silicon Valley remain the centre of much global deal-flow and investment into start-ups and growing companies in this sector.

Switzerland, Malta, Gibraltar

These countries served as early safe havens for ICOs and other novel financial products due to their existing regulatory structures and responsivity to market demand. As a result, there are a large number of blockchain companies domiciled in each of these, even if their development activity occurs outside these borders.

Germany

Berlin appears to be the beating heart of German blockchain activity with a scale of activity to challenge London for the European crown. The range of products under development is also diverse and less financially focused, and the city serves as the global headquarters for Tendermint, IOTA and EOS.

Dubai

Dubai was the first country to step onto the world stage and announce its intention to apply blockchain to every aspect of government infrastructure to improve accountability, transparency and service delivery by 2020. It has served as a friendly and responsive jurisdiction to large companies wishing to experiment in this context.

China

Following a rocky touch-and-go relationship with bitcoin from 2012 to 2016 with various phases of permitting and banning cryptocurrency trading, China's approach to blockchain has largely moved beyond financial services to focusing on securing supply chains and e-government. China is still engaging in the exploration of fintech applications, particularly in its southern city of Shenzen which borders Hong Kong, another strong global financial hub alongside London, Singapore and New York.

Accessing the blockchain ecosystem

An understanding of the shape of the blockchain economy, its continued focus on financial services, its growing interest in data sharing and its global epicentres for development activity, opens the way to tapping into relevant trends.

There is a global shortage of developers, but a vast range of exciting young companies with products to demonstrate across a range of underlying blockchain platforms. The sentiment at the moment within traditional industry remains one of scepticism with few visibly successful projects. But for those willing to engage with cutting edge technology, the focus appears to be on growing consortia of partners ready to collaboratively engage across a common platform. The rules for successfully managing such consortia remain to be seen, but the emergence of the group behind Facebook's cryptocurrency, Libra, has driven this global conversation forward.

The best part of the blockchain ecosystem has always been its openness. This does mean that it attracts a wide range of personalities from across the political spectrum, but the early get-rich-quick attitude from 2013 to 2017 seems to have subsided. There is a sense of common exploration and altruism, which is likely to remain for a few years at least, until clear leaders and dominant platforms emerge. These may not be any of the existing groups, and there is still much scope for black swans to make an appearance with novel legal, technical, or other innovations to satisfy questioning customers.

Accessing this ecosystem is therefore a combination of deciding your own business or personal goals, and reaching out. Local meet-up groups can be found in many places to help with initial education and exploring the paths taken by others. Leading universities will also often have professors or groups exploring the fundamental technology within their business or computing departments.

Accessing the blockchain builders is certainly possible, but many of their interactions occur on software development platforms or in online chat rooms, given the distributed nature of these groups. But they may be hesitant to educate newcomers or discuss potential business relationships due to their focus on the technology. Companies building dApps will also be focused on delivering for existing customers, but potentially open to genuine business interests that don't stray too far from their main goals.

The easiest route to approach professionals in the space will usually be the consultancies who can develop proofs of concept to help customers test ideas and recommend other points of contact.

Finally, there are frequent conferences on blockchain technology across the world. These can provide an easy way to gain insights into the technical and regulatory issues in this space, current thinking about developing and growing systems, and presentations by innovative companies.

Overall, the blockchain ecosystem is broad, generally communicative and looking for business. This can provide a vital way of accessing experts in order to test and develop your own interests in the space.

Dr Robert Learney is head of distributed systems at Digital Catapult. He is involved in developing new programmes to help groups of companies from multiple sectors explore the potential of this technology to unlock economic growth for the United Kingdom. Prior to joining the Catapult, Rob co-founded the Imperial College Centre for Cryptocurrency Research and Engineering in 2014, aiming to create a cross-disciplinary academic focal point for blockchain research in London, and has been following developments across this sector ever since.

18.

RULES FOR
BLOCKCHAIN VENTURES

From hundreds of blockchain projects, ten lessons have emerged for how best to start and manage them, report Thomas Hartmann and Elke Kunde at IBM

Lessons from hundreds of blockchain projects worldwide, based on private, permissioned implementations of Hyperledger Fabric, have been brought together in two IBM publications: *The Founder's Handbook*, a guide to getting started with blockchain, and *Blockchain as a Force for Good*, which identifies five guiding priciples for building trust and real value. Here are the highlights.

For founders of blockchain networks

Identify the business problem

Don't start with 'I'd like to do something with blockchain'.

Pick an existing business problem where multiple parties are involved and frictions exist whose elimination would be beneficial for all involved. Identify the root causes of the pain points and match to a blockchain with the capabilities on which your benefits depend. Start small with a minimum viable product to check the technology fit. Then go ahead with a pilot to prove the business case and model for your solution.

Build your ecosystem

Be clear about the business network you'd like to build: participants, assets and transactions. Define the roles or capabilities that other participants should bring to the table: a design thinking workshop is a good foundation to define functionalities and stakeholders. Think about business models and determine incentives and shared value for the participants.

Business model design

Evaluate the level of permissioning needed for your ecosystem and business processes. As a lot of business rules are coded in smart contracts, the validation criteria and endorsing participants are key for automated secure transactions. The rules must be clear to everyone. Talk about investments and calculate the value together early to make sure that everybody makes a positive return. And think how the benefits change, and for whom, if more participants join or more use cases are added to the business network. It is not a one-time exercise.

Governance

Governance models are still evolving. Incentives for participation and for good behaviour are the foundation of a sustainable business network. But in some cases the incentives do not align and there is a need for mechanisms for co-ordination on top. Governance has two important areas: for the business rules (solution governance) and for the technological aspects (blockchain governance). For example, be clear about how to grow the network in terms of participants and functionality.

Legal considerations

Get legal counsel and experts on data protection/privacy involved early when building a blockchain application. Your application has to comply with respective regulations to become productive. Talk about the ownership and use of intellectual property in the network, as well as liability, and the countries where you intend to operate, as the rules may differ.

As a bottom line, to make blockchain real for business, it's necessary to bring together your ecosystem and find the shared value for participants in your network.

Principles for trust and value in blockchain

Open is better

Consider open technologies and governance models with defined approaches for sharing contributions and try to avoid proprietary technologies.

Permissioned doesn't mean private

Permissioned blockchain does not mean private: it may be open to any party willing to register. Working with identities and permissions is key to regulatory responsibilities and to foster trust among the participants when transacting on a joint platform.

Governance is a team sport

Enterprise blockchains must embrace distributed and transparent governance, preventing undue concentrations of influence. Trust anchors, ie, members who run nodes in the network and participate in transaction validation, should be distributed among multiple participants, taking into account the business rules and funding model. An advisory board of ecosystem participants can help govern the growing network.

Common standards are common sense

Enterprise blockchains should be architected around common standards with interoperability in mind, including deployment models like a cloud platform. The technology will evolve to support a network of networks. Consider defining and publishing your data model and your policies for change. APIs (application programme interfaces) can then be used with permissioned access.

Privacy is paramount

Participants in an enterprise blockchain must be able to control who can access their data and under what circumstances. The rights to the data that reside on a blockchain network should always belong to the creator. Done correctly, even competitors in an industry can work on the same network or platform.

Thomas Hartmann is an expert consultant with IBM Services, working as lead for blockchain in financial services for IBM Global Business Services in the DACH market (Germany, Austria and Switzerland). Thomas has over 25 years of experience in transforming the banking industry with a particular focus on payments and on back office operations in transaction banking at banks and market infrastructures. He got involved in blockchain in 2015 when the fit of the technology for enterprise use was taking its first important steps and is keen on keeping the focus where it adds tangible advantages to end users over 'conventionally digital' bank offerings.

Elke Kunde is an IT architect with IBM Germany's enterprise technical sales, acting as blockchain technical focal point for IBM in the DACH market (Germany, Austria, Switzerland). She is representing IBM Germany as an expert in blockchain standardisation at the German DIN, as well as ISO/TC 30 (blockchain and electronic distributed ledger technologies) and Bitkom's blockchain working group. Elke has more than 20 years' experience in various roles in technical sales for IBM clients in banking, financial markets and insurance.

For further reading, see: *Blockchain for Dummies,* 3rd IBM Edition at https://www.ibm.com/downloads/cas/ OK5M0E49; *The Founder's Handbook* at https://www. ibm.com/downloads/cas/GZPPMWM5; and *Blockchain as a force for good* at https://www.ibm.com/downloads/ cas/AGL5ZWLN.

19.

WHAT MAKES A GREAT
BLOCKCHAIN PROJECT

Troy Norcross at Blockchain Rookies reviews how and where blockchain projects work best

The key to finding the best use cases for blockchain is to look beyond your enterprise. Blockchain adds the most value when the network allows for multiple parties to come together and agree to utilize a single source of truth of core information. The trick is not technology. The trick is to find alignment across multiple stakeholders within an industry and then to identify the incentives to make the project happen. The technology of blockchain and distributed ledger technology (DLT) is the easy part.

Multiple distrusting parties

Business transactions today typically involve one or more third parties acting as brokers or intermediaries to provide trust where it may not exist. These third parties include banks, brokers and dealers. They add value by connecting various parties in a transaction. They also add cost and delays. In some cases, these intermediaries can be the source of errors and even fraud.

Blockchain networks offer the environment for trust to exist without the existence of a third-party brokering the relationship. This trust comes from the fact that all parties can see all information related to transactions in which they are participating. Blockchain also provides the ability to automate business logic between parties with smart contracts reducing conflict and improving the liquidity of a supply chain.

The challenge with blockchain and DLT today is that there are limitations of speed and performance that do not apply to traditional database systems. Many enterprise leaders and IT departments are sceptical when they cannot see a reason to use a conventional database.

If your project is internal and does not involve any external participants, then you may not benefit from blockchain. If you are looking to streamline your supply chain or similar network, but your enterprise is still the primary beneficiary and will control the network, it is again likely that you use a conventional system.

If you have multiple parties working together where many of them are competitors, including competitors to your enterprise, this is the basis for thinking about how blockchain could add value. The best blockchain use cases solve industry problems for multiple enterprises. The best opportunities involve various distrusting parties where no single enterprise is the sole beneficiary nor sole controller of the network.

Single source of truth

Blockchain ledgers and smart contracts can provide a substantial benefit by reducing the costs of reconciling various data sets from multiple parties. If all members of the network agree to use a single source of truth, there is no longer a need for spending the time and money to reconcile your information against that of everyone else in the network of suppliers and partners.

Transparency is a hot topic in blockchain. The bitcoin and ethereum protocols create a public and permissionless network where participants are unknown and where all information is publicly available. Understandably, it might not work for enterprises and enterprise transactions. There are sound business reasons why various aspects of transactions should be kept private except between relevant parties.

Today there are multiple blockchain protocols, including both Hyperledger Fabric and Corda, which allow for private communication between select parties, while still maintaining the advantages of a single source of truth.

Standardization is another crucial aspect to blockchain projects. Part of today's reconciliation process is to adjust the data before attempting to reconcile. For blockchain projects, there is additional work required to agree on standards for information written into the blockchain.

Having a single source of truth which is accessible to relevant parties and utilizing an agreed set of standards makes for the basis for a great blockchain project.

Recognize and align incentives

As well as standards for information and transactions between multiple distrusting parties, it is important to align incentives for each of the participants. As a retailer, for instance, there is an economic incentive to provide end consumers with clear information about the provenance of a product as well as methods of manufacturing, transportation and distribution. The rest of the network may be resistant to joining the network either due to the costs associated or because they benefit from a certain level of opacity in the way they do their business. So what problems could blockchain solve for the rest of the network members?

Liquidity and value added

Today there are significant delays in finance liquidity across the supply chain. Extended payment terms of 60, 90 or even 120 days make for good business sense for the company at the top of the chain, but financing their supply chain is costly for the rest of those downstream. With blockchain and smart contracts, payments can be fully automated according to mutually agreed terms and rules. When using a globally accepted cryptocurrency, payments can be completed faster and for lower fees as well. By improving liquidity, there is value for more participants.

There may be members of networks who no longer add sufficient value to justify their fees. With blockchain and DLT there is a reduced need for intermediaries, brokers and other go-betweens. By eliminating these unneeded parties, the value of former fees returns to the network.

Technology proof

With a solid idea as to how to reduce reconciliation costs and eliminate fees from unnecessary intermediaries, now is the time to start thinking about how to get started with the technology.

There are numerous options for blockchain protocols, each having unique advantages and challenges. Examples of protocols are ethereum, Hyperledger Fabric, Corda and EOS. After protocols, it is essential to select the right architecture for the network, ensuring that nodes (individual computers) are located optimally for network security and meeting business requirements for distribution and decentralization.

Rather than attempt to build a blockchain network from scratch, there are numerous services where you can access a blockchain network hosted and pre-configured for you: BaaS (blockchain as a service). These environments make it easy to get started right away and also to have long-term management and maintenance of the network handled for you.

A significant element of a new blockchain project is understanding how the network will integrate with your existing and legacy data and infrastructure systems. In most cases, enterprises will not replace legacy systems with blockchain, but will instead replace some functions (like reconciliation) and will require integrating the existing systems to read and write from the new blockchain network. The integration aspect of a new blockchain project is one of the most important, and often little appreciated, elements of a successful pilot.

Have a bigger vision

After proof of concept, a blockchain project will give you the foundation for understanding how the technology works, the capabilities and limitations of the network, and how it can truly add incremental business value to your organization.

Remember, the best blockchain projects are more significant than a single enterprise and more expansive than just a supply chain for a single retailer. When you decide to take the project to the next stage, it works best when you have a broader vision in mind on how to involve multiple stakeholders and competitors for when the project grows.

With vision comes an opportunity for leadership. And equally, with vision comes an opportunity for risk. To date, the few cross-industry blockchain projects currently gaining traction have been started by large global multinationals with both vision and an appetite to take risk.

The IBM Food Trust began with Walmart as the core customer and then it grew to more than 50 partners, including one of its biggest competitors. TradeLens started with the Danish shipping company Maersk as the driving force. Today three of the top four maritime shipping companies are using Tradelens meaning that 60 percent of all goods shipped by sea can take advantage of it.

In each of these cases, no single enterprise owned the blockchain platform. Instead, a consortium or foundation owns and operates the project with each participant bringing technology or other resources as part of their participation.

A non-profit organization or consortium governs and directs the project. There is no single entity to make billions from the blockchain network. All participants both contribute and receive value proportionately.

Cross-industry blockchain projects are significant endeavours. In many cases, it is difficult to find a single enterprise to begin because 'no one wants to go first'. While that is true, an extended version of the statement is equally valid, 'no one wants to go first, but the leaders'.

Summary

Blockchain provides an environment where multiple distrusting parties can come together and agree on a single source of truth and a single source for automated business logic (smart contracts). Identifying the right blockchain projects begins with looking at your business and broader challenges across your industry.

If you are looking for ways to reduce costs of reconciliation and unnecessary intermediaries, reduce friction and fraud in your supply chain, provide your consumers with provenance and traceability for products in your industry, then blockchain may be the basis for a solution to transform your entire industry.

Troy Norcross is co-founder of Blockchain Rookies and former chief executive of Opengoods. Focusing on the business opportunities created by blockchain, Troy separates the value from the technical delivery of blockchain projects. With a background ranging from software development for flight simulators to running his own start-up focused on permission marketing, Troy has a wealth of experience across multiple industries. Hailing originally from 4000 acres of farmland in Missouri, Troy has lived in Amsterdam, Munich, Helsinki and currently resides in London. Troy's breadth of experience provides a unique perspective when looking at how blockchain can be applied to a business opportunity or to an industry at large.